understanding MICROECONOMICS

For NCEA Level Three

EXTERNALS/INTERNALS

Dan Rennie

Workbook RESOURCE

Understanding Microeconomics for NCEA L3
1st Edition
Dan Rennie

Typeset by : *Book*NZ

Any URLs contained in this publication were checked for currency during the production process. Note, however, that the publisher cannot vouch for the ongoing currency of URLs.

For product information and technology assistance,
in Australia call **1300 790 853**;
in New Zealand call **0800 449 725**

For permission to use material from this text or product, please email **aust.permissions@cengage.com**

National Library of New Zealand Cataloguing-in-Publication Data
A catalogue record for this book is available from the National Library of New Zealand

ISBN 978 0 17 043811 7

Cengage Learning Australia
Level 7, 80 Dorcas Street
South Melbourne, Victoria Australia 3205

Cengage Learning New Zealand
Unit 4B Rosedale Office Park
331 Rosedale Road, Albany, North Shore 0632, NZ

For learning solutions, visit **cengage.co.nz**

Printed in China by 1010 Printing International Limited
7 8 9 10 25 24

Contents

A digital version of the *Teacher Resource*, which contains full answers to this workbook, is available via Vital Source for only $19.95 for 12 months.

For more information:

Email: nz.sales@cengage.com

Website: www.cengage.co.nz.

1 MICRO-ECONOMIC CONCEPTS
Marginal utility and demand

Utility and demand

As people consume goods or services they gain satisfaction (termed **utility**). Utility is measured in units of satisfaction termed utils. **Total utility (TU)** is the aggregate satisfaction gained from consuming successive quantities of a good. **Marginal utility (MU)** is the change or additions to total utility resulting from consumption of one extra unit of a good or service. MU equals TU2 minus TU1.

When making purchases, rational consumers aim to maximise their total satisfaction. If a consumer finds that the consumption of a good or service provides less satisfaction or utility than the price they paid to obtain the good or service, then this is not a rational or wise decision.

Tony Gordon's utility schedule for chewing gum each day		
Quantity consumed (packs)	Total utility (TU) (cents)	Marginal utility (MU) (cents)
1	80	80
2	144	64
3	192	48
4	224	32
5	244	20
6	244	0
7	230	−14

Tony Gordon's demand schedule for chewing gum each day	
Price (cents)	Quantity demanded (packs)
80	1
64	2
48	3
32	4
20	5
0	6

From the table we can observe that if a consumer's purchases increase, then the marginal utility will decrease. Therefore if a consumer was to decrease his or her purchases of a product, then marginal utility would increase.

As more of a product is consumed (as shown in the table), total satisfaction (total utility) increases but this will be at a decreasing rate. This is known as the **law of diminishing marginal utility**, that is, as more of a good or service is consumed holding all else constant, total utility increases but at a decreasing rate.

The rational consumer attempting to maximise his or her total utility should purchase more goods until price **(P) equals MU**; this is the **optimum purchase rule**. The individual demand curve is derived from the individual's marginal utility (MU) curve, because consumers receive less extra satisfaction as consumption increases they will only buy more of a good or service if the price falls. Therefore, the demand curve will slope downwards to the right. It follows that a rational consumer who finds that the price of a good or service was greater than the additional satisfaction (MU) obtained from consuming it, will decide it was not worth buying the good or service.

A demand schedule can be derived from a utility schedule. Marginal utility determines the price consumers are willing to pay for a good or service. When constructing a demand schedule or graph using a utility table the quantity is taken from the quantity figure given while the corresponding marginal utility figure is the price that consumers are willing to pay. For example, Tony is willing to pay 80 cents for the first packet of chewing gum and 64 cents for the second packet. The price he is willing to pay for each additional packet of chewing gum matches the falling marginal utility in the table.

    ISBN: 9780170438117

Consumer equilibrium – two or more goods

To maximise total utility with limited income a consumer will be in equilibrium where MU Good A/Price Good A = MU Good B/Price Good B = MU Good C/Price Good C. This is where the marginal utility spent on the goods or services is equal.

Kyle's utility table						
	Movies ($10)			Pizza ($5)		
Quantity	TU	MU	MU per dollar	TU	MU	MU per dollar
1	100	100	10	70	70	14
2	180	80	8	130	60	12
3	230	50	5	170	40	8
4	250	20	2	200	30	6
5	260	10	1	210	10	2

Kyle has an income of $35 and is deciding on which combination of pizza ($5 each) and movies ($10 each) will give him the highest total utlity and therefore the greatest satisfaction. His equilibrium is where the MU of Pizza/Price of Pizza equals MU of Movies/Price of Movies. In this instance it will be three pizzas and two movies. At this equilibrium Kyle's total utility is 350 utils (170 utils plus 180 utils), there is no other combination of pizza or movies that would result in a higher total utility for Kyle.

The order of purchases of pizza and movies is dependent on the MU per dollar. Kyle will purchase the products with the highest MU per dollar given his limited income. The first purchase is therefore a pizza because it has a MU per dollar of 14 (70/$5), next is another pizza because it has a MU per dollar of 12 (60/$5). Next is a movie because the MU per dollar is 10 (100/$10). The next purchase will be either a pizza or movie because the MU per dollar for both is 8. Kyle will be indifferent to consuming either, and since Kyle has $35 to spend he is able to purchase both.

Student notes: Marginal utility and demand

   ISBN: 9780170438117

Consumer equilibrium – two or more goods

_____

_____

_____

_____

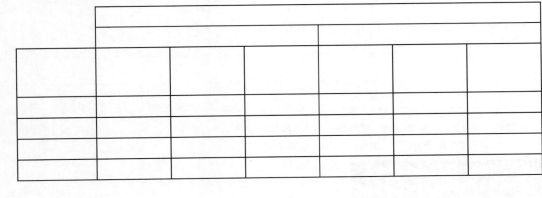

_____

_____

_____

_____

_____

_____

_____

1 a Explain the difference between total utility and marginal utility.

_____

_____

_____

b Explain the law of diminishing marginal utility.

_____

_____

_____

c Complete the table that shows Ian's total and marginal utility from buying cans of soft drink per week.

Quantity consumed (cans)	Total utility (cents)	Marginal utility (cents)
1	200	
2	360	
3	460	
4		64
5		40

d Use the concept of marginal utility to explain why the demand curve for the product slopes downward.

_____

_____

_____

_____

e Use the information in the table above to complete Ian's demand schedule for cans of soft drink per week and draw a demand curve in the grid provided.

Ian's demand schedule for cans of soft drink per week	
Price (cents)	Quantity demanded

2 a Complete the table and use it to complete the sentences.

Quantity consumed (pies)	Total utility	Marginal utility
0	0	
1	24	24
2		20
3	56	
4	60	

A decrease in the amount of a good purchased would _____ total utility, and marginal

utility will _____.

b Look at the values in the marginal utility column above and state the law of economics they show.

_____

_____

c State the optimum purchase rule.

_____

d State the consumer equilibrium rule (or formula) a consumer should use to ensure they maximise total utility they receive from purchasing two products.

_____

e The price of good A is $2 and the price of good B is $1.50. If a consumer evaluates the marginal utility of B to be 30 and he or she is in equilibrium with respect to purchases of A and B, then he or she must consider the marginal utility of A to be what?

_____

f Explain the significance of the law of diminishing marginal utility in deriving the individual demand curve.

_____

_____

_____

_____

g Indicate if the following statements are correct or incorrect.

(i) The consumer gains the maximum utility for the money available when the quantity purchased is at a point where P > MU.

_____

(ii) The consumer gains the maximum utility for the money available when the quantity purchased is at a point where P = MU.

_____

(iii) When a consumer increases consumption of a good or service the MU tends to decrease and they will be prepared to pay less.

_____

(iv) The consumer's equilibrium occurs when the marginal utility per dollar of all goods and services is equal (this is the equi-marginal rule).

_____

3 Alan is a Year 13 Economics student who likes drinking flavoured milk. Explain the concept of utility. In your answer you should:

- Complete the table below by calculating the missing values.
- Draw Alan's demand schedule for flavoured milk per day in the schedule provided.
- Define the law of diminishing marginal utility.
- Explain, using the law of diminishing marginal utility, why Alan's demand curve will slope downwards to the right. Refer to the table in your answer.

Alan's utility schedule for flavoured milk (per day)		
Number of bottles consumed	Total utility (cents)	Marginal utility (cents)
1	600	
2	1 000	
3		300
4	1 500	
5		100

_____
_____
_____
_____
_____
_____
_____
_____
_____
_____
_____
_____

     ISBN: 9780170438117

4 Mark Cambo enjoys hitting golf balls and often goes to the driving range to hit a basket of golf balls. He gives you the following information about his utility.

Explain the concept of utility. In your answer you should:

- Complete the table below by filling in the missing numbers.
- Plot Mark Cambo's demand curve for golf balls on the grid below.
- Name the law that explains why Mark gains less satisfaction with every basket of balls purchased.
- Use marginal utility to explain why Mark Cambo purchases more baskets of golf balls when the price of a basket of golf balls falls.

Mark Cambo's utility schedule for baskets of golf balls		
Quantity consumed (basket of balls)	Total utility (cents)	Marginal utility (cents)
1	600	
2		400
3	1 200	
4		50

_____
_____
_____
_____
_____
_____
_____
_____
_____
_____
_____
_____

5 Julian likes to hire videos or video games at the local store. Videos are $10 each and video games $8.

a Complete the table given.

Quantity of each product	Marginal utility of videos (utils)	MU per $ videos	Marginal utility of video games (utils)	MU per $ video games
1	80		56	
2	40		40	
3	20	2	32	
4	10		24	

b State the law of economics that the changing values of marginal utility show in the table.

_____

_____

c State the consumer equilibrium rule Julian needs to apply to maximise the total utility he receives from buying videos and video games.

_____

_____

d How many videos and video games should Julian purchase to maximise his total utility?

Number of videos _____

Number of video games _____

e Explain using the optimum purchase rule why Julian would buy fewer videos if their price increased.

_____

_____

_____

_____

_____

_____

_____

_____

_____

_____

_____

_____

_____

              ISBN: 9780170438117

6 A consumer, Jacob, assigns the following utility to successive levels of consumption.

Units consumed	Utility					
	Pizza	MU per $	Drink	MU per $	Wedges	MU per $
1	120		22		40	
2	90		20		36	
3	60		18		32	
4	40		14		28	
5	20		12		24	
Price per unit	$10		$2		$4	

Help Jacob maximise the total utility he receives from purchasing pizza, drinks and wedges. In your answer you should:
- Complete the MU per $ column for each product in the table.
- State the consumer equilibrium rule (or formula) Jacob should use to ensure he maximises the total utility he receives.
- Assume Jacob has $20 to spend. What combination of goods will he buy?
- In what order will Jacob purchase pizza, drinks and wedges? Justify your answer for Jacob's fifth purchase.

_____
_____
_____
_____
_____
_____
_____
_____
_____
_____
_____
_____
_____
_____
_____
_____
_____
_____
_____
_____

Price elasticity of demand

Price elasticity of demand (Ep) measures the responsiveness of quantity demanded of a good or service to changes in its price.

Inelastic demand (ep < 1)

Goods or services that are inelastic in nature have the following characteristics, they tend to have **no, or few, close substitutes** and are often considered **necessities**, for example bread, milk, medical services. The products may be **addictive**, such as cigarettes or alcohol. When the relative cost of the commodity is a **small fraction of total spending** then demand will be inelastic, for example a newspaper.

For goods or services that are inelastic in nature (Ep < 1) **a given change in price causes a less than proportionate change in quantity demanded**. As the price of a product increases total revenue will increase, while a price decrease will cause total revenue for firms to decrease.

Inelastic demand curve

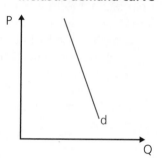

Elastic demand (ep > 1)

Goods and services that are **elastic** in nature have the following characteristics:-they tend to have **many substitutes** and are often considered **luxuries** such as designer clothing, eating out at a five star Michelin restaurant or staying in a penthouse suite at a hotel. When the relative cost of the commodity is a **high proportion of total spending** then demand will be elastic, for example a new car.

For goods and services that are elastic in nature (Ep > 1) **a given change in price causes a more than proportionate change in quantity demanded**. As the price of a product increases total revenue for a firm will decrease, while a price decrease will cause total revenue for firms to increase.

Elastic demand curve

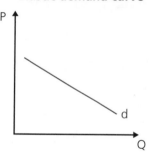

Tax and elasticity

The incidence of a tax refers to who actually pays the tax. In most cases, part of a tax is paid by the consumer and part is paid by the firm. The incidence of a tax falls mainly on consumers when a good or service is inelastic. When demand is inelastic, a given increase in price will see a less than proportionate decrease in quantity demanded, meaning that producers are more able to pass on most of the tax to consumers. Consumers pay to the extent of the price rise, this will be the greatest incidence of the tax. Any amount of the tax not covered by the price increase has to be absorbed by the firm.

Taxes placed on goods that are price inelastic can raise significant revenue. The reason for this is that the price rise caused by the imposition of the tax on goods or services that are inelastic in nature will cause a proportionately small decrease in quantity demanded. This results in a relatively large number of goods or services on which the tax is imposed, and therefore greater tax revenue is collected. Given this, a government is more likely to impose taxes on products such as cigarettes and alcohol that are inelastic in nature, than products such as new cars.

Taxes placed on goods that are price elastic may raise less revenue than a tax placed on goods that are price inelastic. The reason for this is that the price rise caused by the imposition of the tax on goods or services that are elastic in nature will cause a proportionately large decrease in quantity demanded. This can leave only a relatively small number of goods or services on which the tax is imposed, and therefore less tax revenue is collected.

Calculating price elasticity of demand

Price elasticity of demand can be calculated using the revenue method, which compares the change in price (P) with the change in total revenue (TR). Total revenue (TR) equals price (P) multiplied by the quantity sold (Q). If a firm desires to increase revenue it would increase price if the product was inelastic in nature and decrease price if the product was elastic in nature.

Revenue method for price elasticity of demand			
Price change	Inelastic EP < 1	Unitary Ep = 1	Elastic Ep > 1
P ⬆	TR ⬆	TR ⬌	TR ⬇
P ⬇	TR ⬇	TR ⬌	TR ⬆
	TR/P changes are in the same direction	TR remains the same with price changes	TR/P changes are in the opposite direction

Midpoint method

The midpoint method to calculate price elasticity of demand (Ep) uses the averages of the quantity demanded and price to work out the elasticity coefficient.

To calculate the price elasticity of demand using the midpoint method, the following formula is used (the change in quantity demanded/the midpoint of the quantity demanded) divided by (the change in price of/the midpoint of the prices indicated). Note the final number (coefficient) will always be a negative number because price and quantity demanded always occur in opposite directions. To be strictly accurate the coefficient should be written as a negative number. However, it is common practice in economics to ignore the negative sign.

For example, the price of coffee rose from $15 per kg to $20 per kg and sales fell from 100kg to 80kg per week. The price elasticity of demand for coffee equals (−20/90) divided by ($5/$17.5) is −0.777 which is 0.78, therefore the price elasticity of demand for coffee is inelastic.

$$Ep = \cfrac{\left[\cfrac{\text{change in quantity demanded}}{\text{midpoint of quantity demanded}}\right]}{\left[\cfrac{\text{change in price}}{\text{midpoint of the prices indicated}}\right]} = \cfrac{\left[\cfrac{\dfrac{\Delta Qd}{Q1 + Q2}}{2}\right]}{\left[\cfrac{\dfrac{\Delta P}{P1 + P2}}{2}\right]}$$

Price elasticity of demand is a point concept so a demand curve can have a range of elasticities, typically relatively elastic (Ep greater than 1) at the top end and relatively inelastic (Ep less than than 1) at the lower end.

A demand curve for X

$$Ep = \frac{(2/4)}{(-2/11)} = -2.75$$
$$= 2.75 \text{ elastic}$$

$$Ep = \frac{(3/11.5)}{(-3/3.5)} = -0.30$$
$$= 0.30 \text{ inelastic}$$

Student notes: Elasticity of demand

_____

_____

_____

_____

_____

_____

_____

_____

_____

_____

_____

_____

_____

_____

_____

_____

_____

_____

_____

_____

_____

_____

_____

_____

_____

_____

_____

_____

ISBN: 9780170438117

1 **a** Define price elasticity of demand and give the formula to calculate Ep.

_____

_____

_____

_____

b Work out price elasticity of demand for each question below. Show your working (round to two decimal places). Use the midpoint method.

(i)

Price ($)	Quantity demanded
1.50	100
1.70	95

_____

_____

(ii) Work out the Ep on the curve at the positions indicated.

Ep is _____

Ep is _____

c Explain what a price elasticity of demand coefficient of less than one indicates about a good or service.

_____

_____

_____

_____

_____

_____

_____

_____

_____

2 Calculate price elasticity of demand for each of the following questions (to two decimal places). Work out Ep using the midpoint method.

a

_____

_____

b

	Price $	Quantity demanded
Old situation	25	100
New situation	30	60

_____

_____

c Complete the table.

Relative changes in price/revenue	Elasticity – unitary, inelastic, elastic
(i) Price increases and total revenue remains unchanged	
(ii) Price increases and total revenue increases	
(iii) Total revenue increases when price rises from $10 to $12	
(iv) P ↓ TR ↓	
(v) P ↓ TR remains the same	
(vi) Price decreases and total revenue increases	
(vii) TR ↑ when price falls	
(viii) Revenue remains the same when price falls	
(ix) Change in price and total revenue are in the same direction	
(x) TR ↑ P ↑ or P ↓ TR ↓	
(xi) Changes in TR and P go in the opposite direction	

d (i) Give reasons why the price elasticity of demand coefficient of wiper blades is 0.19.

_____

_____

_____

(ii) Indicate what will happen to a firm's revenue if they increase the price. Explain why.

_____

_____

_____

       ISBN: 9780170438117

3 a Indicate the price elasticity of demand indicated by the situation outlined in the table below.

Situation		Elasticity of demand
(i)	The response to a given change in price is an exactly proportionate change in quantity demanded	
(ii)	The response to a given change in price is a more than proportionate change in quantity demanded	
(iii)	The response to a given change in price is a less than proportionate change in quantity demanded	
(iv)	Price elasticity of demand is greater than 1	
(v)	%Δ price < %Δ quantity demanded	
(vi)	%Δ price = %Δ quantity demanded	
(vii)	%Δ QD < %Δ price	

b Doctor visits fell from 10 000 to 9 000 when price increased from $25 to $30. What is the price elasticity of demand for doctor visits? Give a possible reason for doctor visits, relating it to the Ep you calculated.

_____

_____

c The brewery decides to increase the price of a jug of beer from $4.50 to $5.00 and the quantity sold decreases from 7 500 to 7 300.

   (i) Work out the change in revenue from the price increase. Was this an increase or decrease in revenue?

   _____

   _____

   _____

   (ii) Work out Ep using the midpoint method.

   _____

   _____

d Explain what a price elasticity of demand coefficient of greater than one indicates about a good or service.

_____

_____

_____

_____

_____

_____

_____

4 Price elasticity of demand is a point concept.

Explain price elasticity of demand using the graph below. In your answer you should:

- Define 'price elasticity of demand'.
- Calculate price elasticity of demand along the demand curve. Use the midpoint method and show your working.
- Describe how a knowledge of price elasticity will assist a firm to increase total revenue.

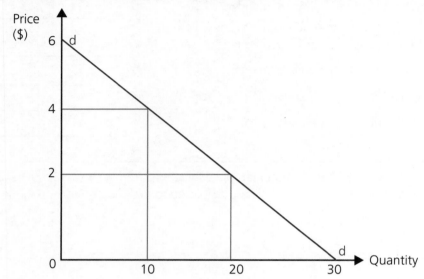

_____

_____

_____

_____

_____

_____

_____

_____

_____

_____

_____

_____

_____

_____

_____

_____

_____

_____

_____

_____

5 Various factors determine the price elasticity of demand for a product. The demand coefficient of water is 0.15, coffee 0.56 and meals out at a restaurant 1.35. Firms use this knowledge in their pricing decisions.

Explain factors that determine price elasticity of demand and how firms use this knowledge. In your answer you should:

- Explain factors that influence price elasticity of demand with reference to the information above.
- Explain how firms will use a knowledge of price elasticity of demand in their pricing decisions.

_____

_____

_____

_____

_____

_____

_____

_____

_____

_____

_____

_____

_____

_____

_____

_____

_____

_____

_____

_____

_____

_____

_____

_____

_____

_____

_____

_____

_____

_____

_____

_____

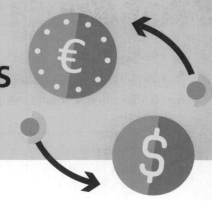

3 MICRO-ECONOMIC CONCEPTS
Elasticity of supply

Price elasticity of supply

Price elasticity of supply (Es) measures the **responsiveness of quantity supplied** of a good or service to **changes in price**.

Supply over time

Supply curves over time

Momentary supply is supply at a given point in time and is sometimes referred to as supply on a given day. The quantity supplied is fixed regardless of price (illustrated by the perfectly inelastic supply curve shown, drawn as a vertical line). The curve reflects that firms have only a fixed amount of stock on hand available to meet demand and are **unable to alter any factors**, for example tickets to a school social, or the lots available for sale at an auction. There is no responsiveness in the quantity supplied to a change in price and the coefficient of elasticity of supply is zero.

In the **short-run time period, at least one input is fixed**. The firm is restricted in its ability to change output. In the short run the supply of all goods is inelastic because the quantity supplied is limited to the quantity of finished goods on hand or easily available. Supply **elasticity** is said to **lower**.

In the **long run period** firms have **time to expand their use of all factors** and so increase their total output capacity. Shortages and profits will attract more firms to the industry, which will increase total market supply. Over time, supply will be more responsive to price (elastic) as existing producers are able to increase production levels, new producers can enter the market, and improvements in technology increase productivity. **Elasticity** is then said to be **higher**.

Supply is inelastic, or relatively unresponsive to price changes in the short run, and elastic, or relatively responsive, in the long run. In response to a price change output will change by more in the long-run than short-run time period, as shown in the diagram above.

Factors that determine elasticity of supply

Manufacturers who are able to quickly increase (decrease) output in response to higher (lower) prices because they are able to have longer (shorter) production runs with an increase (decrease) in overtime have a more responsive elasticity of supply. A company that has excess capacity should be able to increase its output without a rise in costs. In this situation the supply curve is elastic because it can respond to changes in demand. When economies are in recession it is assumed that resources (land, capital and labour) are not being fully utilised and elasticity can be higher.

       ISBN: 9780170438117

The **ability** of a firm to be able to **store stock (inventory)** influences the elasticity of supply. If a company has finished products in stock it is able to respond quickly to increases in demand, therefore supply will be elastic. The opposite applies when there is less inventory, in this situation supply will be more inelastic.

The longer the duration that a firm is allowed to adjust its production levels the more elastic the supply curve is. However, agricultural producers tend to have either inelastic supply or momentary supply (perfectly inelastic) because producers have made decisions about what crops to plant and have limited land, further they are often subject to climate conditions that influence output.

Calculations price elasticity of supply

$$Es = \dfrac{\left[\dfrac{\text{change in quantity supplied}}{\text{midpoint of quantity supplied given}}\right]}{\left[\dfrac{\text{change in price}}{\text{midpoint of the prices indicated}}\right]} = \dfrac{\left[\dfrac{\Delta Qs}{\dfrac{Q1 + Q2}{2}}\right]}{\left[\dfrac{\Delta P}{\dfrac{P1 + P2}{2}}\right]}$$

The midpoint method to calculate price elasticity of supply (Es) uses the averages of the quantity supplied and price to work out the elasticity coefficient.

To calculate the price elasticity of supply using the midpoint method, the following formula is used (the change in quantity supplied / the midpoint of the quantity supplied) divided by (the change in price / the midpoint of the prices indicated).

For example: the price of X increases from $9 to $11 and quantity supplied increases from 300 to 500. The price elasticity of supply equals (200/400) divided by ($2/$10) equals 2.50, therefore the price elasticity of supply for X is elastic.

A supply curve for Y

$$Es = \dfrac{(3/10.5)}{(3/11.5)}$$
$$= 1.10 \text{ (elastic)}$$

$$Es = \dfrac{(1/4.5)}{(2/3)} = 0.33 \text{ (inelastic)}$$

Price elasticity of supply is a **point concept** so a supply curve can have a range of elasticities, typically relatively elastic (Es greater than 1) at the top end and relatively inelastic (Es less than than 1) at the lower end. When price elasticity of supply equals one it is termed unitary.

When **price elasticity of supply is less than one** this means that a **given change in price causes a less than proportionate change in quantity supplied** and indicates **inelastic supply** (Es less than one).

When **price elasticity of supply is greater than one** this means that **a given change in price causes a more than proportionate change in quantity supplied** and indicates **elastic** supply (Es greater than one).

Student notes: Price elasticity of supply

Elasticity of supply

_____

_____

_____

_____

_____

_____

_____

_____

_____

_____

_____

_____

_____

_____

_____

_____

_____

_____

_____

_____

_____

_____

_____

_____

_____

_____

_____

_____

_____

_____

_____

_____

_____

_____

_____

QUESTIONS & TASKS

1 **a** Define 'price elasticity of supply'.

_____

_____

b Work out the price elasticity of supply for each question below (show your working). Use the midpoint method.

(i)

Price ($)	Quantity supplied
1.00	17
0.95	10

_____

_____

_____

(ii) Work out the Es on the curve at the positions indicated.

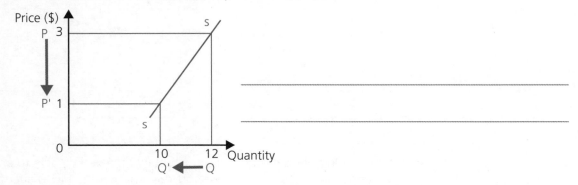

_____

_____

_____

c Use the diagram to match up the curves with the description below. Write the letter of your choice.

Relatively inelastic supply _____

Demand curve _____

Momentary supply curve – on a given day _____

Relatively elastic supply _____

d Complete the table below.

Situation	Elasticity
(i) The response to a given change in price is a more than proportionate change in quantity supplied.	
(ii) The response to a given change in price is a less than proportionate change in quantity supplied.	
(iii) A given price change causes no change in quantity supplied.	
(iv) %Δ price > %Δ quantity supplied	
(v) %Δ quantity supplied > %Δ price	

2 Calculate the price elasticity of supply for each question below (show your working). Use the midpoint method.

a

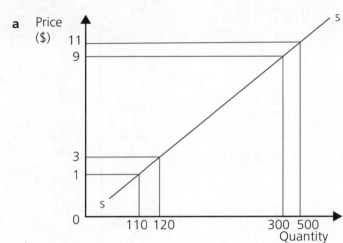

(i) Between $11 and $9:

_____

_____

(ii) Between $3 and $1:

_____

_____

b Briefly explain why there is a difference in the short-run and long-run supply curves for bottled water.

_____

_____

_____

_____

_____

_____

c Complete the table using the following phrases and ideas; momentary time period, able to alter all factors, the firm has at least one fixed factor, long-run, short-run, a firm is unable to alter any factors, A, B and C.

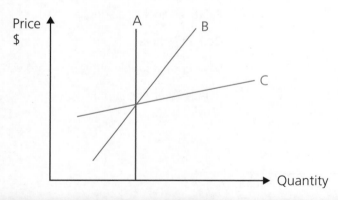

Supply elasticity	Curve	Features	Time period
Es > 1			
Es < 1			
Es = 0			

3 a Below are the correct supply curves in the short-run and long-run time periods. Use these graphs and your own knowledge to complete the sentences that follow.

Supply in the short run

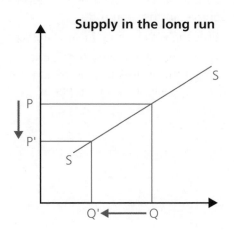

Supply in the long run

(i) Supply in the short run is relatively _____ and in the long run relatively _____.

(ii) 'In response to a price _____ the output will fall by more in the _____ run than it does in the _____ run.'

(iii) In the short run supply is relatively _____ and in the long run more _____.

(iv) Supply on a given day is _____ _____ and the curve is drawn as a _____ line.

(v) When a given price change causes a more than proportionate change in quantity supplied this indicates _____. The short-run supply curve is relatively _ _____.

(vi) Inelastic supply occurs when a given change _____ _____. The long-run supply is relatively _____.

b Calculate price elasticity of supply for each question below (show your working). Use the midpoint method.

(i)

_____

_____

(ii)

Price ($)	Quantity supplied
1.00	30
1.50	34

_____

_____

4 Supply over time

Supply is inelastic, or relatively unresponsive to price changes in the short run, and elastic, or relatively responsive, in the long run.

Explain supply over time. In your answer you should use diagrams and:

- Explain the momentary time period.
- Explain the short-run time period.
- Explain the long-run time period.

_____

_____

_____

_____

_____

_____

_____

_____

_____

_____

_____

_____

_____

_____

_____

_____

_____

_____

_____

_____

_____

_____

_____

_____

_____

_____

_____

_____

ISBN: 9780170438117

5 Alfred Marshall developed the economic theory that price elasticity of supply for a good or service is linked to time periods.

Graph 1: The market supply of fish

Explain price elasticity of supply. In your answer you should:

- Define price elasticity of supply and explain the difference between inelastic and elastic supply.
- Assume that fish prices have increased. With reference to Graph 1, explain which of the three supply curves for fish is most appropriate for a period of one year. Justify your answer.

_____

_____

_____

_____

_____

_____

_____

_____

_____

_____

_____

_____

_____

_____

_____

_____

_____

_____

_____

_____

4 MICRO-ECONOMIC CONCEPTS
Diminishing returns and supply

Inputs in the production process

Resources (or factors of production) are the economic inputs used by producers in the production process. Resources can be classified as natural resources, capital goods, human resources and entrepreneurship. Depending on the business some factor inputs are unable to be changed in the short run and are considered to be fixed, other factor resources or inputs are able to be used in greater quantities, these would be considered to be variable inputs in the production process. However, in the **short run** every firm will have **at least one fixed factor**. This could be skilled workers (human resources) or the land (natural resources) used in the production process. For firms involved in manufacturing, the fixed input in the production process is most likely to be the building (factory, office or premises) from which the firm operates. It could also be other capital resources such as equipment, machinery or vehicles. The variable input that may be easier for some firms to change in the short run could be the ability to hire or employ additional workers or the ability to use more raw materials or power. In the **long-run** firms **can change all inputs** (the factors of production) and the firm can be more adaptable and change the size of its operations.

Diminishing returns

The law of **diminishing returns** refers to the idea that as more and more of a factor (input) is used, with at least one fixed factor, there is some point at which the increase in output will be at a decreasing rate.

Diminishing returns occurs in the **short run** when there is **at least one fixed input** and the **increase in a firms output is at a decreasing rate**. In the table, we assume that workers are the only variable factor in the production process. The first worker adds 10 units to total output, the second worker adds 20 units to total output and the third worker adds 10 units to total output. Diminishing returns set in after the second worker (with the employment of the third worker). The additions to output (marginal output) increased between the first and second workers, thereafter the additional output falls as diminishing returns set in.

Firms will experience diminishing returns in the short run because, in the short run, at least one factor input is fixed. If additional quantities of other (variable) factors are added into the production process, the total output will increase at a diminishing rate (marginal product must eventually fall). This is because each factor has less of the fixed factor to work with, reducing its ability to produce (extra) output.

Workers	Total output	Marginal output
1	10	10
2	30	20
3	40	10
4	46	6
5	48	2
6	46	−2

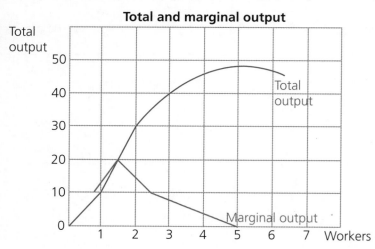

Diminishing returns will cause a firm's marginal costs to increase because as each additional variable unit produces less when diminishing returns are occurring, **the production of extra units of output will require more and more of variable inputs to produce them** (compared with earlier units). Therefore, it follows that the cost of each additional unit produced (i.e., MC) must increase because more inputs are being used to produce it. So, marginal cost must rise as output increases.

Increasing returns to a factor reflect that a firm's short-run average costs would be falling. The increased input of a factor results in increasing additions to output, or a decreased input results in a smaller decrease in output. If a firm decreases an input by 5% but output falls by only 4%, the addition to outputs is actually increasing. The production process must be more efficient than before and costs must be falling (in the short run).

Decreasing returns to a factor (or diminishing returns) reflect that the increase of one input results in decreasing additions to output. The firm increases an input by 5% but output rises by only 3%. Similarly a decrease in an input would result in a larger decrease in output. An input falls by 10% and output decreases by 12%. Both these examples show that the production process has become inefficient. The short-run average costs (SAC) will eventually rise.

Break-even and shut-down points for a firm

Break-even and shut-down points

Break-even is the **price** at which **revenue covers all economic costs**. On the graph the value of break-even is shown as the value of Pb ($4.5). The two cost curves equal to the price at the break-even point are the marginal cost curve and average cost curve (MC and AC).

Between Pb and Ps a firm is operating below its break-even point and above its shut-down point. It has a price which covers all its average variable costs (AVC) and is paying some of its fixed costs. It should continue producing in the short run because if it shuts-down it still must pay fixed costs.

Shut-down is the **price** where **revenue just covers variable costs**. Shut-down is shown as the value Ps on the graph ($2). The shut-down point is at a level where price is just equal to average variable costs (AVC). At this point the firm is indifferent to whether it continues to produce or shuts-down. The two cost curves equal to the price at the shut-down point are the marginal cost curve and average variable cost curve (MC and AVC).

Firms will shut down if the price falls below the minimum average variable cost (AVC). At any price below its minimum average variable cost, a firm is not covering its variable costs or making any contribution to fixed costs. Therefore, a firm is better off by shutting down and ceasing operations. It will no longer use variable inputs (raw materials, power) and therefore no longer have to pay any variable costs but will still have to pay fixed costs from some other source.

Fixed costs (FC) are independent of output, they must be paid whether or not the firm is producing, e.g., rent, mortgage repayments, rates. These are costs that a firm cannot avoid and must pay because they involve contractual arrangements with other parties, even if the firm has closed down (ceased producing). **Variable costs (VC)** represent costs directly related to production and if there is no production, variable costs are zero, for example, power, raw materials, postage, wages. As a firm starts producing a firm will begin to incur and pay variable costs.

Deriving the supply curve from the marginal cost curve

Supply is the amount of a good/service producer's offer for sale at each price (ceteris paribus). **Marginal cost** is the addition to total cost resulting from the production of an extra unit of output. A firm will only offer a good/service for sale if the price they receive covers the cost of producing it (i.e., the marginal cost).

Deriving the supply curve from the MC curve

A firm's supply schedule from the MC curve	
Price	**Quantity supplied**
1.00	0 (zero)
2.00	200
4.50	300
8.00	400

At $8 the quantity supplied is 400 and at $3 the quantity supplied is 240 because the marginal cost curve (MC) above AVC or shut-down is a firm's supply curve. At $1 the quantity supplied is zero (0) because the price is below the shut-down point and the firm has ceased operating and is not producing.

The firm's **short-run supply curve** is derived from the marginal cost curve and starts from the minimum of the average variable cost curve. A firm's short-run supply curve is that part or portion of the **marginal cost curve above AVC (or shut-down)**.

The short-run supply curve for a firm

Since a firm's supply curve is the marginal cost curve, it will shift to the right (outward) if costs decrease or shift to the left (inward) if costs increase.

Student notes: Diminishing returns and supply

_____

_____

_____

_____

_____

_____

_____

_____

_____

QUESTIONS & TASKS

1 **a** Explain why firms experience diminishing returns in the short run.

_____

_____

_____

_____

_____

b Explain why diminishing returns cause a firm's marginal costs to increase.

_____

_____

_____

_____

_____

c For each table indicate when diminishing returns sets in **(i)** after the … **(ii)** with the ….

Output	10	100	250	450	550
Machines	1	2	3	4	5

(i) after the _____ **(ii)** with the _____

Output	20	50	90	150	250	260	265
Workers	1	2	3	4	5	6	7

(i) after the _____ **(ii)** with the _____

Machine	Output
1	50
2	150
3	160
4	165
5	167

(i) after the _____ **(ii)** with the _____

d Why does the marginal cost curve initially fall and then rise?

_____

_____

_____

       ISBN: 9780170438117

Output	200	300	400	500	600
Marginal costs	30	25	60	78	100

2 Explain the relationship between ouput and marginal costs. In your answer you should:

- Draw a sketch diagram of a marginal cost curve and explain its shape.
- Explain why diminishing returns cause a firm's marginal costs to increase.
- Describe the relationship between marginal cost and the quantity supplied of a product by a firm.

_____

_____

_____

_____

_____

_____

_____

_____

_____

_____

_____

_____

_____

_____

_____

_____

_____

_____

_____

_____

_____

_____

_____

_____

_____

_____

_____

_____

_____

3 Use the diagram to answer the questions below.

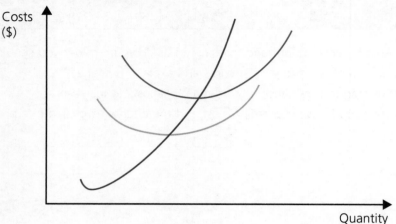

a Label the curves and identify and label the break-even and shutdown points.

   (i) What is the vertical distance between AC and AVC equal to? _____

   (ii) Is this gap a constant? _____

   (iii) When the firm is not producing it must still pay what types of costs? _____

   (iv) What costs are directly related to production? _____

   (v) If the firm is not producing, what is the value of these costs? _____

b Write fixed costs or variable costs for the following terms.

Rent   _____   Wages   _____

Raw materials _____   Debt servicing   _____

Interest   _____

c What is debt servicing?

_____

_____

d Define the following terms.

Break-even: _____

Shutdown: _____

e Complete this statement.

If a firm ceases its operation it must still pay _____ costs. If market price is above the level of

average variable cost, it can cover its _____ costs and still have something left over to pay

its fixed costs, it may as well _____ operating. If price falls below AVC, there is nothing

left over to contribute to _____ costs and variable costs are not fully covered, then the firm

should _____

 ISBN: 9780170438117

4 a Write if the following statements are correct or incorrect.

(i) A firm's supply curve is equal to its AC curve. _____

(ii) A firm's supply curve is equal to its MC curve above AVC. _____

(iii) When revenue covers all economic costs it is at shutdown. _____

(iv) Break-even is when revenue covers variable costs only. _____

(v) At any revenue below shutdown, the firm will save paying variable costs

by not operating but will still have to pay fixed costs. _____

(vi) Break-even is when revenue covers all economic costs. _____

b Label the curves on the diagram and clearly label the break-even point (label B) and the shutdown point (label SD).

c Give the value of: **(i)** Shutdown _____ **(ii)** Break-even _____.

d What cost concept is represented by the vertical gap between AVC and AC? _____

e Why does this gap narrow as output rises?

_____

_____

_____

_____

_____

_____

f Which two cost curves are equal to the price at:

(i) shutdown point? _____ **(ii)** break-even point? _____

g Explain why the firm can continue producing in the short run at $0.70.

_____

_____

_____

_____

Total and marginal product for the Smoked Meat Company

5 Explain the relationship between diminishing returns and a firm's marginal costs.
In your answer you should
- State when diminishing returns set in, after/with.
- Explain why firms experience diminishing returns in the short run.
- Explain why diminishing returns cause a firm's marginal costs to increase.

_____

_____

_____

_____

_____

_____

_____

_____

_____

_____

_____

_____

_____

_____

_____

_____

_____

_____

_____

_____

6 The average variable cost curve is important in determining the short-run supply curve for the perfectly competitive producer.

Explain the relationship between a firm's average variable cost curve and its supply curve. In your answer you should:

- Label the curves in Graph one and complete the supply schedule next to it.
- Label the shutdown point (label S) and break-even point (label B) on Graph one.
- Define the terms break-even and shutdown and indicate which two cost curves are equal to the price at each point.
- Explain how a firm's supply curve is derived from MC

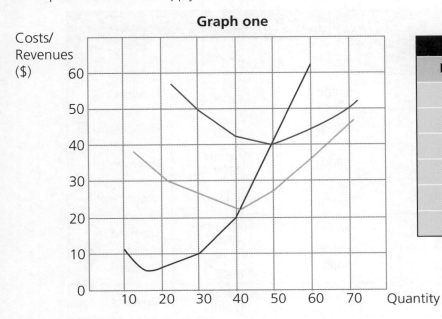

Graph one

Costs/ Revenues ($)

Supply schedule	
Price ($)	**Quantity**
10	
20	
30	
40	
50	
60	

_____

_____

_____

_____

_____

_____

_____

_____

_____

_____

_____

_____

_____

_____

_____

_____

_____

_____

_____

MICRO-ECONOMIC CONCEPTS
Role of prices:
Market equilibrium

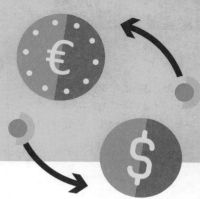

Establishing market equilibrium

Market for pizza weekly				
Price $	Quantity demanded	Quantity supplied	Market situation	Pressure on price
14	0	12000	Surplus 12000	Downward
12	2000	10000	Surplus 8000	Downward
10	4000	8000	Surplus 4000	Downward
8	6000	6000	Equilibrium	None/Stable
6	8000	4000	Shortage 4000	Upward
4	10000	2000	Shortage 8000	Upward
2	12000	0	Shortage 12000	Upward

Equilibrium is a term to denote a balance between forces involved. The **equilibrium price and equilibrium quantity** in a market is determined by the interaction of the forces of demand and supply. Equilibrium in a market is the price at which the quantity demanded by consumers equals the quantity supplied by producers. At the equilibrium, both parties involved in the market are completely satisfied, with consumers having purchased all they want to buy, and producers having sold all they want to sell.

At the market equilibrium the **market will clear** and there will be neither a surplus (excess supply) or a shortage (excess demand). Therefore, all stock is sold (i.e., no stock is unsold) and consumers do not want to buy any more of the good or service. As long as the conditions of demand and conditions of supply remain unchanged (ceteris paribus) then the equilibrium price and equilibrium quantity will remain unchanged.

On a schedule the equilibrium can be found where the quantity demanded by consumers and the quantity supplied by producers are equal at one particular price.

On the diagram, the equilibrium price for pizza is $8 (Pe) and the equilibrium

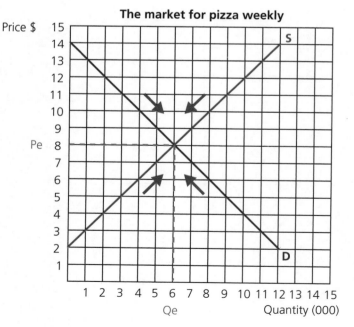

quantity for pizza is 6 000 (Qe) because this is where the demand curve and the supply curve intersect, with the quantity demanded by consumers equal to the quantity supplied by firms.

ISBN: 9780170438117

Shortage (excess demand)

A **shortage (excess demand)** will occur at any price below the equilibrium where the quantity supplied by producers is less than the quantity demanded by consumers. When there is a shortage the market will react with consumers bidding up the price. As the price of a good or service increases quantity supplied increases because selling the good or providing that service becomes relatively more profitable for firms because the revenue (income) they earn is higher and firms will be more able to cover costs. As the price of a good or service increases consumers' real incomes fall and the good or service becomes relatively less affordable, consumers will be less willing and able to purchase the good or service with their limited incomes and look to buy more of a relatively cheaper substitute.

A shortage of 8 000 will occur at $4 (P1) because at this price the quantity supplied by producers (Qs, 2 000) is less than the quantity demanded by consumers (Qd, 10 000). As price increases the quantity demanded by consumers decreases from 10 000 (Qd) to 6 000 (Qe), while the quantity supplied by producers increases from 2 000 (Qs) to 6 000 (Qe). Equilibrium is restored at $8 (Pe) where quantity supplied equals quantity demanded of 6 000 (Qe) and the market clears.

The market for pizza weekly

At any price below the equilibrium the quantity sold in the market equals the quantity supplied by producers. There is no unsold stock at any price below the equilibrium.

Surplus (excess supply)

A **surplus (excess supply)** will occur at any price above the equilibrium where the quantity supplied by producers is greater than the quantity demanded by consumers. When there is a surplus the market will react with firms willing to accept a lower price to get rid of unsold stock. As the price of a good or service decreases quantity supplied decreases because selling the good or providing that service becomes relatively less profitable for firms because the revenue (income) they earn is lower and firms will be less able to cover costs. As the price of a good or service decreases consumers' real incomes rise and the good or service becomes relatively more affordable, consumers will be more willing and able to purchase the good or service with their limited incomes and look to buy less of a relatively more expensive substitute.

A surplus of 4 000 will occur at $10 (P2) because at this price the quantity supplied by producers (Qs, 8 000) is greater than the quantity demanded by consumers (Qd, 4 000). As the price decreases the quantity demanded by consumers increases from 4 000 (Qd) to 6000 (Qe), while the quantity supplied by producers decreases from 8 000 (Qs) to 6 000 (Qs). Equilibrium is restored at $8 (Pe) where quantity supplied equals quantity demanded of 6 000 (Qe) and the market clears.

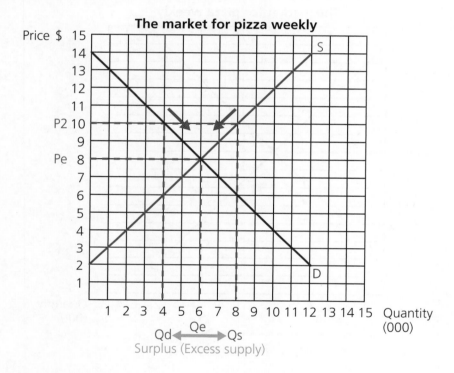

At any price above the equilibrium the quantity sold in the market equals the quantity demanded by consumers. The quantity of the stock unsold in the market equals the size of the surplus.

Shortage (excess demand) and shifts of the demand and/or supply curves

A shortage (excess demand) will occur where the quantity supplied by producers is less than the quantity demanded by consumers. When the condition of ceteris paribus is relaxed and there is either an increase in demand (an outward shift of the demand curve) and/or a decrease in supply (an inward shift of the supply curve), this will create a shortage (excess demand) at the original price.

The market will react to a shortage with consumers bidding up the price. Price rises, until equilibrium price and quantity is reached and the market clears.

A decrease in supply

Surplus (excess supply) and shifts of the demand and/or supply curve

A surplus (excess supply) will occur where the quantity supplied by producers is greater than the quantity demanded by consumers.

When the condition of ceteris paribus is relaxed and there is either a decrease in demand (an inward shift of the demand curve) and/or an increase in supply (an outward shift of the supply curve), this will create a surplus (excess supply) at the original price.

When there is a surplus, firms will accept a lower price to get rid of unsold stock. The price falls, until the equilibrium price and quantity is reached and the market clears.

An increase in supply

Student notes: Role of prices: market equilibrium

     ISBN: 9780170438117

1 At a price of $6.00, the market supply of DVD movies each week is 250. As the price falls to $5.00 the quantity supplied falls by 20%. If the price is $2.00 the supply is 100 and 120 at $3.00.

a Draw the market for DVD movie rentals each week from the information provided.

Price ($)	Market demand
6.00	100
5.00	120
3.00	200
2.00	250

b Identify the equilibrium price and quantity. price = _____ quantity = _____

c (i) On your graph, show the market situation if the price of a DVD movie rental was $3.00. Fully label the graph and explain why the price of a DVD is likely to rise in this situation.

_____

_____

(ii) Explain fully how the equilibrium quantity is restored when the price increases. Use the terms 'quantity supplied' and 'quantity demanded' in your answer.

_____

_____

     ISBN: 9780170438117

2 Study the graph and answer the questions that follow.

a Work out the missing quantity supplied and write them in the space provided.

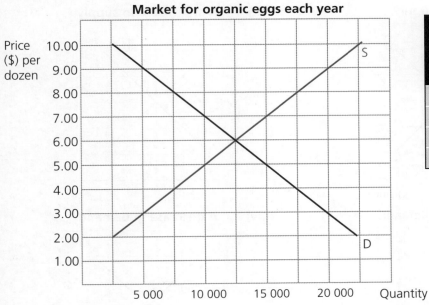

Market for organic eggs each year

Price $ per dozen	Fresh eggs quantity supplied	Natures Ways quantity supplied
2.00	1 000	
4.00	3 250	
8.00		11 000
9.00		12 000

b What is the equilibrium price and quantity?

Price _____ Quantity _____

c Identify the price where a surplus of 5 000 will occur. Also identify at this price the quantity demanded and the quantity supplied.

Price _____ Quantity demanded _____ Quantity supplied _____

d How will the market react to a surplus of 5 000?

_____

_____

_____

_____

_____

e Explain how the quantities for a market supply curve are derived.

_____

_____

_____

f Explain why firms supply more as the price increases.

_____

_____

_____

_____

3 a Draw the change indicated by the TITLE of each graph and label each diagram fully. Label the original price and quantity as P and Q respectively. Label the new price and quantity as P' and Q' respectively.

(i)   A decrease in supply

(ii)   An increase in supply

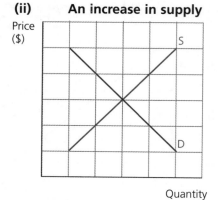

(iii)   An increase in demand

(iv)   A decrease in demand

b Write 'demand' or 'supply' for each idea below depending on what condition each statement represents. The first one is done for you.

(i)	income is a condition of	demand	**(ix)**	price of a substitute is a condition of	
(ii)	sales tax is a condition of		**(x)**	price of a complement is a condition of	
(iii)	subsidy is a condition of		**(xi)**	GST is a condition of	
(iv)	tariff is a condition of		**(xii)**	indirect tax is a condition of	
(v)	advertising is a condition of		**(xiii)**	direct tax is a condition of	
(vi)	cost of raw materials is a condition of		**(xiv)**	productivity is a condition of	
(vii)	technology is a condition of		**(xv)**	flood, strike, disease is a condition of	
(viii)	fashion/taste is a condition of		**(xvi)**	price of a related good is a condition of	

c Complete the table.

Situation	Causes
(i) Shift of demand curve to the right	
(ii) Shift of supply curve to the right	

4 a Students are encouraged to bring their own laptops, smartphones or tablets to use in schools. Show the change this has had on the market for smartphones. Label the new equilibrium price and quantity as P1 and Q1 respectively.

New Zealand market for smartphones

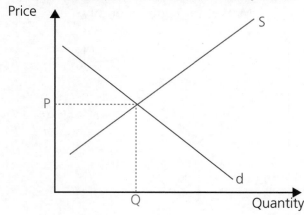

b (i) State the situation that would exist in the market if the price remained at the original equilibrium P.

_____

(ii) Explain the market forces that result in the new equilibrium price and quantity, at P1 and Q1.

_____

_____

_____

_____

_____

_____

_____

c (i) There has been a decrease in the cost of coal extraction. Use the sketch graph below to show the effect of this decrease on the market for coal.

Market for coal

(ii) Explain how equilibrium is restored after the change.

_____

_____

_____

_____

_____

_____

_____

_____

_____

_____

_____

> The health benefits of eating apples has just been published in a medical journal, they contain a range of vitamins.

5 a On the graph below, show the impact that is likely to result from the resource material above. Use dotted lines to show the new price and quantity. Fully label the changes.

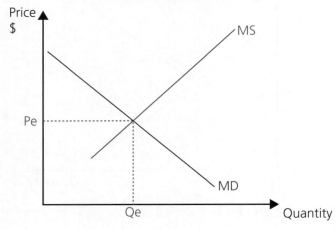

Market for apples monthly

b Discuss how this information affects market demand. In your answer you should explain how market demand is determined and explain the effects this report will have on market demand.

_____

_____

_____

_____

_____

_____

_____

_____

_____

_____

c Discuss the effect this change will have on the market for apples monthly.
In your answer you should:
- explain the effect on apple consumers
- explain the effect on apple producers.

_____

_____

_____

_____

_____

_____

_____

_____

_____

_____

_____

Sunrise and sunset industries

A firm is a single business while an industry is the sum of all firms which produce one type of product. The dairy industry in New Zealand includes all those firms involved in producing dairy products for sale from the farmers who milk cows, firms who process the milk into final or intermediate products, and firms who market the final product.

If prices for dairy products in world markets rise, the industry as a whole will prosper and grow. Dairy farmers will be encouraged to invest more in milk production. For example, farmers may purchase land, converting sheep farms to dairy production. This will involve the purchase of capital items such as milking sheds, tractors and equipment. Milk production will increase, farmers' incomes will rise and they may employ extra workers.

Factories processing milk and firms marketing the final product will also increase output and sales. Employment will rise and spending will increase beyond the dairy industry.

The hospitality and travel industry may well benefit as individuals with increased disposable incomes take holidays and travel. Regions whose economies are dependent on the dairy industry are likely to benefit the most from the expansion in economic activity.

As domestic and global economies go through the trade cycle of recession, recovery and boom, it is likely that the part of the trade cycle that the New Zealand economy is in will differ from a number of its trading partners. If there is a downturn in overseas demand, there are likely to be reduced incomes and possibly business closures for firms that rely heavily on export orders. Unemployment is likely to rise and living standards in the affected areas and communities will be lower.

The converse applies for a recovery and increase in overseas demand. While some industries may be experiencing a decline in activities it is possible that other industries are experiencing growth, e.g., while the car and shoe manufacturing industries have declined, other industries such as tourism, wine, education and dairying have grown in size and importance in the New Zealand economy.

The changing demand for a product in local or world markets may be temporary or permanent. Resources will switch from declining industries (**sunset**) into growth industries (**sunrise**) where prospects and profits are likely to be better.

There is always likely to be a change in the fortune of various industries within an economy at any given point in time. The change will mean some individuals losing jobs in some industries, while new opportunities arise in other industries, some firms' profits declining while others are growing, firms may close down or may go through a process of restructuring.

Student notes: Role of prices and profits

    ISBN: 9780170438117

QUESTIONS & TASKS

Government economic reform and changes in domestic and international demand patterns have transformed the New Zealand economy. Businesses have shifted from old 'sunset' industries to innovative 'sunrise' industries.

1 a Indicate if the following industries are 'sunset' or 'sunrise' industries.

(i) boat building _____ **(ii)** organics _____

(iii) car manufacturing _____ **(iv)** wine _____

(v) education _____ **(vi)** tourism _____

(vii) film making _____ **(viii)** shoe manufacturing _____

(ix) dairying _____ **(x)** wool and sheep _____

b The difficulty with economic reform is the short-term losses, and long-run gains. Outline some possible short-term losses and long-run gains that were a result of reform policies that liberalised trade in New Zealand.

(i) Short-term losses: _____

_____

_____

_____

(ii) Long-term gains: _____

_____

_____

_____

c Indicate if the following statements are facts or opinions. Justify your answers.

(i) A 'sunset' industry will always be a 'sunset' industry. _____

_____

_____

(ii) The growth and contraction of some New Zealand industries will depend on what goes on in the global economy. _____

_____

_____

_____

_____

2 The ski industry continues to grow as more tourists visit during the New Zealand winter.
Explain the impact of the ski industry on the New Zealand economy. In your answer you should:
- Explain the effect of increased tourist numbers on the ski industry in New Zealand.
- Explain the effect on prices and profit.

3 Foreign fee-paying student numbers continue to decline as the recession continues and the dollar appreciates.

Explain, using the education industry, the effect on an industry when it is in decline. In your answer you should:

- Explain the effect on providers of education.
- Explain the flow-on effects to other industries, profits and resource use.

_____

_____

_____

_____

_____

_____

_____

_____

_____

_____

_____

_____

_____

_____

_____

_____

_____

_____

_____

_____

_____

_____

_____

_____

_____

_____

_____

_____

_____

_____

Consumer surplus (CS)

Consumer surplus (CS) is the difference between the maximum amount that a person is willing to pay for a good or service and its current market price. It represents the benefit consumers receive over and above what they actually pay (Pe) for a good or service. The earlier units purchased provide more satisfaction (utility) than the price paid.

On the diagram, consumer surplus is the shaded area because consumers only pay the market equilibrium price (Pe) for all purchases (of a hard copy book), therefore they enjoy a surplus in terms of what they would be willing to pay (demand) rather than go without on the earlier units. To calculate the value of consumer surplus, it is the value of the area above the equilibrium price paid (Pe) and below the demand curve, i.e. the shaded triangle on the diagram PeAP5. The area of a triangle equals a half (0.5) multiplied by the base multiplied by the height. In this instance the value of consumer surplus equals 0.5 multiplied by 3m books multiplied by $10 which equals $15m.

The value of consumer spending (or expenditure) equals the price paid (Pe) multiplied by the quantity purchased (Qe), $40 multiplied by 3m books which equals $120m. The value of total utility or satisfaction from the consumption of Qe units, is the area QeAP50 which equals $135m.

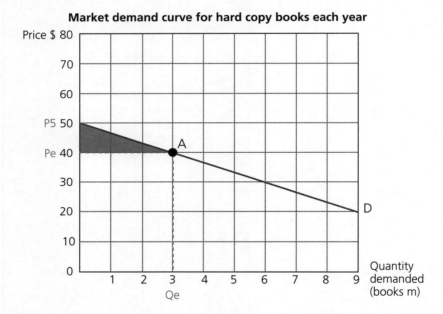

Market demand curve for hard copy books each year

If the market equilibrium price fell to $30 per book the new quantity demanded would increase to 6m books. The new value of consumer surplus would be 0.5 multiplied by 6m books multiplied by $20 which equals $60m, because this is the area above the new price paid and below the demand curve. The change in consumer surplus would be an increase of $45m because this is the difference between the value of the original consumer surplus ($15m) and the value of the new consumer surplus ($60m). In this instance, consumer surplus on the original quantity is greater because equilibrium price has fallen. Since the quantity consumed has increased there are more units on which the consumer derives a surplus.

Producer surplus (PS)

Producer surplus (PS) is the difference between the total earnings of suppliers for a certain quantity sold and the total costs required to put that quantity on the market. Producer surplus occurs in the market for a good or service because firms are willing to supply each unit for a lower price than they receive in the market.

On the diagram, producer surplus is the shaded area because while producers receive the market equilibrium price (Pe) for all units sold they are willing to supply each unit for a lower price than what they are paid. To calculate the value of the producer surplus, it is the value of the area below the price firms receive (Pe) and above the supply, i.e. the triangle PeAP1. The area of a triangle equals a half (0.5) multiplied by the base multiplied by the height. In this instance, the value of producer surplus equals 0.5 multiplied by 3m books multiplied by $30 which equals $45m.

The total revenue received by the producer for Qe units is the price they receive (Pe) multiplied by the quantity sold (Qe), $40 multiplied by 3m books equals $120m. The total cost to the producer to supply Qe units is the area below the supply curve P1AQeO, which is $75m.

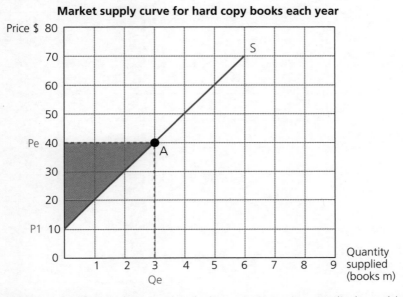

Market supply curve for hard copy books each year

If the market equilibrium price fell to $30 per book the new quantity supplied would decrease to 2m books. The new value of producer surplus would be 0.5 multiplied by 2m books multiplied by $20 which equals $20m, because this is the area below the new price received and above the supply curve. The change in producer surplus would be a decrease of $25m because this is the difference between the value of the original producer surplus ($45m) and the value of the new producer surplus ($20m).

Student notes: Consumer surplus/producer surplus

_____

_____

_____

_____

_____

_____

_____

_____

_____

_____

_____

_____

_____

_____

_____

_____

_____

_____

_____

_____

_____

_____

_____

_____

_____

_____

_____

_____

_____

       ISBN: 9780170438117

QUESTIONS & TASKS

1 a Draw up the demand curve of the schedule below.

Annabelle's demand schedule for new release DVDs each month	
Price ($)	**Quantity demanded**
10.00	11
11.00	9
12.00	7
13.00	5
14.00	3
15.50	0

b Why does Annabelle buy more new release DVDs as the price falls?

_____

_____

c List two causes (other than changing the price of substitutes for DVDs) that could shift the demand curve for DVDs to the right, i.e., increase the demand for DVDs. For each cause, give the reason to explain why the demand curve will shift to the right.

_____

_____

_____

_____

_____

d What is demand? _____

e Explain why an increase in price does not result in a decrease in demand.

_____

_____

f Assume the market price is $12, calculate the value of:

(i) Consumer spending _____

(ii) Consumer surplus _____

g Shade in the area of consumer surplus at $12.

2 **a** **(i)** Use the diagram to calculate consumer surplus for both demand curves at a price of $10. Show your working.

Demand for a product

CS at Demand _____

CS at Demand 1 _____

(ii) Calculate the value of consumer spending for both demand curves.

_____

_____

b Use the demand curve shown to complete the table below. Show your working.

Jim's demand curve for restaurant meals each year

Quantity demanded

Price $	Value of consumer spending	Value of consumer surplus
(i) 25		
(ii) 50		
(iii) 100		

c Define consumer surplus.

_____

_____

_____

 ISBN: 9780170438117

3 a Draw the supply curve for paperback books given the schedule below.

Supply schedule for paperback books each month	
Price ($ per book)	Quantity supplied
2	0
12	5 000
24	7 000

b (i) Define producer surplus.

_____

_____

_____

_____

(ii) Describe the effects of a change in price of paperback books each month from $2 per book to $12 per book. Relate your answer to the change in producer surplus.

_____

_____

_____

_____

c Calculate producer surplus at a price of

(i) $8 _____

(ii) $10 _____

d Illustrate on your graph an increase in supply. Label fully.

e Explain how the supply curve illustrates the law of supply.

_____

_____

_____

_____

f Define individual supply.

_____

_____

_____

4 As price changes so will consumer spending and consumer surplus.

Explain the statement above with reference to the diagram below. In your answer you should:

- Define consumer surplus and calculate the change shown.
- Calculate the change in consumer spending.

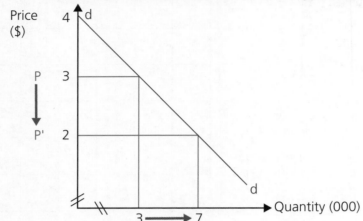

Demand for bottled water each week by consumers

_____

_____

_____

_____

_____

_____

_____

_____

_____

_____

_____

_____

_____

_____

_____

_____

_____

_____

_____

_____

_____

_____

_____

_____

5 Producer surplus (PS) for a firm will change if there is a change in price and/or costs.
Explain producer surplus. In your answer you should refer to the graph and:

- Define supply and producer surplus.
- Calculate producer surplus at a price of $20 and $40.
- Show an increase in supply by 50%. Label this change fully.
- Discuss the resulting change in producer surplus at $20 and $40.

Supply curve for paperback books each month

_____

_____

_____

_____

_____

_____

_____

_____

_____

_____

_____

_____

_____

_____

_____

_____

_____

_____

8 EFFICIENCY OF MARKET EQUILIBRIUM
Allocative efficiency

Allocative efficiency and a production possibility curve

Production possibility curves are drawn on the assumption that there are two goods only, fixed resources and a given level of technology. A **production possibility curve (PPC)** or production possibility frontier (PPF) shows the maximum output combination of two goods that can be produced given that existing resources and technology are used fully, that is, to their best possible use with the least cost.

The maximum output shown by any point on the PPC shows scarcity, because it is impossible to produce beyond the curve with existing resources or state of technology.

For the production possibility curve to shift outwards, the firm or economy needs to find new resources, or develop new technology.

Production possibility curve

Any point inside the curve (for example point D) is production inefficient, which means resources are not being fully utilised or put to their best possible use.

All points on a PPC are production efficient but only one position can be allocatively efficient, that is, it is the position that represents what consumers actually want.

Any point on a PPC frontier shows production efficiency because this is where resources are fully employed and resources put to their best possible use.

The point of **allocative efficiency** is a single point on the production possibility frontier which represents that combination of goods that consumers actually want, or when it is not possible to make someone better off without making someone else worse off.

Any point inside the PPC graph such as D shows that some resources are not fully used; this is termed **production inefficiency**. The economy could possibly have an increase in its standard of living without incurring an opportunity cost.

Allocative efficiency

Allocative efficiency requires production efficiency, and it is not possible for one person to be made better off without making anyone else worse off. This means there is no possible reallocation of resources that will make someone better off without making someone else worse off. Allocative efficiency occurs at the free market equilibrium where the total consumer surplus and the total producer surplus are maximised.

The market system operates automatically to allocate our economic resources to the most efficient socially desirable use, it is said to be allocatively efficient. This point, where the demand curve and supply curve intersect, is the point of allocative efficiency. This is shown in the diagram as point AE. Note, the areas of consumer surplus and producer surplus do not have to be equal. At the market equilibrium price of $40 per book the value of consumer surplus is $15m and the value of the producer surplus is $45m.

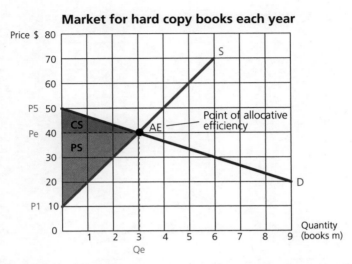

Market for hard copy books each year

If the market automatically shifts away from the equilibrium, the consumer surplus and producer surplus will change and a new allocative efficiency will be established.

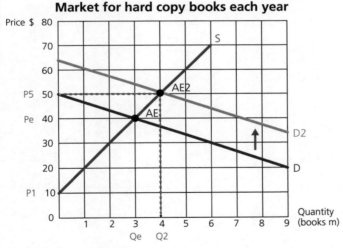

Market for hard copy books each year

If the market equilibrium price rose to $50 per book the value of the consumer surplus and producer surplus will change. The new value of consumer surplus would be 0.5 multiplied by 4m books multiplied by $15 which equals $30m because this is the area above the new price paid ($50/P5) and below the new demand curve (D2). The change in consumer surplus would be an increase of $15m because this is the difference between the value of the original consumer surplus ($15m) and the value of the new consumer surplus ($30m). The new value of producer surplus would be 0.5 multiplied by 4m books multiplied by $40 which equals $80m, because this is the area below the new price received ($50) and above the supply curve. The change in producer surplus would be an increase of $35m because this is the difference between the value of the original producer surplus ($45m) and the value of the new producer surplus ($80m).

Student notes: Allocative efficiency

ISBN: 9780170438117

QUESTIONS & TASKS

1 Allocative efficiency requires production as well as that combination of goods and services that consumers actually want.

Explain allocative efficiency. In your answer you should:
* Explain how the production possibility curve (PPC) in Graph 1 illustrates the concepts of scarcity and opportunity cost.
* Explain how the market would move the economy from Point A to Point B on Graph 1 as peoples' tastes changed from organic flowers to organic vegetables and illustrate the opportunity cost of this change.
* Explain how the move from Point A to Point B on Graph 1 reflects a move from productive efficiency to allocative efficiency.

Graph 1
A production possibility curve for organic crops

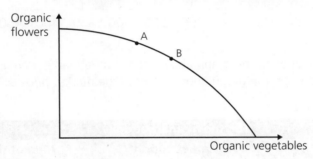

_____

_____

_____

_____

_____

_____

_____

_____

_____

_____

_____

_____

_____

_____

_____

_____

_____

_____

_____

The movie market daily

2 a From the information contained in the graph above, construct a market demand and market supply schedule in the table below. On the graph above, identify the market price as Pe and the market quantity as Qe.

The movie market daily		
Adult price ($)	**Market supply**	**Market demand**
10		
12		
14		
16		

b As a result of increased competition from cheaper DVD rentals, there is a 50% decrease in the number of people going to the movies. Draw a new market demand curve, labelled Md′. Identify the new market price as P1′ and new market quantity as Q1′.

c What is the new equilibrium price and quantity? $ _____

d Complete your table (show your working).

	Original equilibrium	New equilibrium
(i) CS		
(ii) PS		
(iii) Consumer spending		

3 a Explain the difference between consumer surplus and producer surplus.

_____

_____

_____

_____

_____

_____

b Use numbers to indicate the answers asked for.

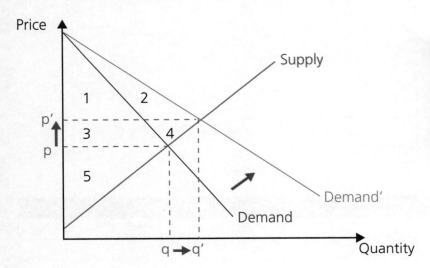

Question	Area
CS before	
CS after	
PS before	
PS after	
Change in PS	

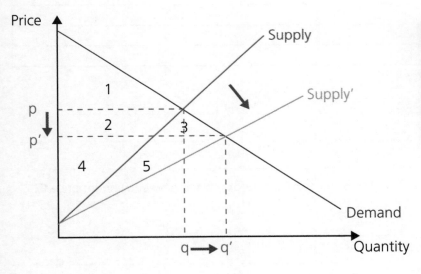

Question	Area
CS before	
CS after	
Change in CS	
PS before	
PS after	

4 Use the graph to answer the following questions.

The market for hardback books

a Complete the table.

Calculate	Working and answer
(i) CS before	
(ii) CS after	
(iii) Change in CS	
(iv) PS before	
(v) PS after	
(vi) Change in PS	

b Define allocative efficiency.

_____

_____

_____

c Explain how market forces move the market for hardback books to the new equilibrium price P1 and quantity Q1.

_____

_____

_____

_____

_____

d Define consumer surplus (CS).

_____

_____

_____

5 Use the graph to answer the following questions.

The market for McKats Combos

a Complete the table.

Calculate	Working and answer
(i) CS before	
(ii) CS after	
(iii) Change in CS	
(iv) PS before	
(v) PS after	
(vi) Change in PS	

b Explain how market forces move the market for McKats Combos back to the new equilibrium price P1 and quantity Q1.

_____

_____

_____

_____

_____

_____

_____

c Define producer surplus (PS).

_____

_____

_____

_____

_____

_____

6 If the market shifts away from the equilibrium, the CS and PS will be reduced and/or redistributed. Fully explain changes in consumer spending and producer surplus. In your answer you should refer to the graph and:

- Explain the changes in consumer surplus, producer surplus and AE.
- Explain how the market forces restore the equilibrium.

The market for crayfish

_____

_____

_____

_____

_____

_____

_____

_____

_____

_____

_____

_____

_____

_____

_____

_____

_____

_____

_____

_____

_____

 ISBN: 9780170438117

7 Resources should be allocated according to consumer demand.

Fully explain how a change in demand will affect consumer surplus and producer surplus. In your answer you should refer to the graph and:

- Define the terms 'consumer surplus' and 'producer surplus'.
- Explain how market forces restore the equilibrium.
- Explain how the change in demand affects CS and PS.

The market for movie tickets

_____
_____
_____
_____
_____
_____
_____
_____
_____
_____
_____
_____
_____
_____
_____
_____

9 EFFICIENCY OF MARKET EQUILIBRIUM
Sales tax and allocative efficiency

Sales tax and allocative efficiency

An **indirect tax** (such as sales tax or VAT) is a tax collected by firms (a third party) and then passed on to the government. An indirect tax will decrease supply causing the equilibrium price to rise and equilibrium quantity to decrease. To **illustrate the effects of a per unit (dollar) sales** tax requires shifting the original supply curve upward to the left by the per unit tax amount. For example, if the per unit tax is $5 and $5 equates to 5 spaces on the graph, you must shift the entire supply curve vertically upwards by this distance. It is important to note that the increase in the price will not be as much as the amount of the tax because the curves are sloping. Therefore, the producer is able to pass some of the tax on to the consumer.

Market for pizza and tax

Consumer Surplus

Producer Surplus

Tax Collected

Deadweight Loss

PE is the original price and QE is the original quantity
P2 is the new price and Q2 is the new quantity
Pp is the price per item firms receive with an indirect tax

The tax per unit is the gap between the supply curves. Note the price does not rise by the full amount of the tax per unit. In this case the tax per unit is $5 but the price has gone up by $4.

	Original equilibrium	New equilibrium
(i) Consumer surplus (CS)	0.5 × 12m × $12 = $72m	0.5 × 8m × $8 = $32m
(ii) Producer surplus (PS)	0.5 × 12m × $3 = $18m	0.5 × 8m × $2 = $8m
(iii) Deadweight loss (DWL)	Nil (zero)	0.5 × 4m × $5 = $10m

With a tax consumer surplus will decrease because consumers pay more and buy less. Producer surplus will decrease because producers receive a lower price and sell less. There is a deadweight loss from the tax that represents the loss of allocative efficiency because part of the original consumer surplus and producer surplus is not picked up as part of the tax.

The impact of a sales tax worked example

	Before the tax	After the tax
Quantity sold	Qe, 12m	Q2, 8m
Price consumers pay	Pe, $4	P2, $8
Consumer spending	Pe x Qe, $48m	P2 x Q2, $64m
Price producers receive	Pe, $4	Pp, $3
Producer revenue	Pe x Qe, $48m	Pp x Q2, $24m
Change in the value of sales	(Pe x Qe) difference (P2 x Q2). An increase of $16m	
Change in producers' revenue	(Pe x Qe) difference (Pp x Q2). A decrease of $24m	
How much is the tax per unit?	The size of the gap between the supply curves. $5	
Government revenue from the tax	Tax per unit x Q2. $5 x 8m = $40m	

The **incidence of a tax** refers to who actually pays the tax. In most cases, part of a tax is paid by the consumer and part is paid by the firm. **Consumers** pay to the extent of the price rise from the original price paid (Pe) to the new price paid (P2). Any amount of the tax not covered by the price increase has to be absorbed by the firm (from Pe to Pp on the diagram opposite).

The change in the value of consumer spending that results from the tax equals the difference between the original price a consumer pays (Pe) multiplied by the original quantity purchased (Qe) and the new price paid (P2) multiplied by the new quantity purchased (Q2). Since a tax results in a price increase there will be a decrease in quantity demanded because fewer consumers are willing and able to purchase with their limited incomes.

The value of consumer spending may remain unchanged, decrease or increase because the new value of consumer spending depends on the relative changes in both the new price paid and the new quantity purchased. Consumers may look to buy a substitute good or service that is relatively cheaper.

Producers will find that the tax adds to their costs so they will decrease supply, meaning that there will be a decrease in quantity supplied at each and every price. The firm will collect the tax revenue and pass this onto the government. Therefore, the price per item firms receive with a tax will be lower than the price consumers pay for them.

To identify how much producers earn per item for the product at the new equilibrium you track down from the new equilibrium position until you hit the original supply curve, this gives the price per item firms receive with a tax (shown on the diagram as the letter Pp).

The change in the firm's income or revenue will be the difference between the firm's original income, which was the original price (Pe) received multiplied by the original quantity (Qe) and the new value of the firm's income, which equals the price per item the firm now receives (Pp) multiplied by the new quantity sold (Q2).The producer's total income with the sales tax will fall because the price per item that the firm receives will be lower and the quantity sold will fall.

The revenue that the **government** collects from the tax equals the tax per unit multiplied by the new quantity (tax per unit x Q2).

The incidence of a sales tax

The **incidence of a tax** refers to who actually pays the tax. In most cases, part of a tax is paid by the consumer and part is paid by the firm.

When the demand curve is relatively inelastic the producer is able to pass on most of the tax to the consumer as shown in the diagram. The shaded area is the consumer incidence of the tax.

The incidence of a tax falls mainly on consumers when a good or service is inelastic. When demand is inelastic, a given increase in price will see a less than proportionate decrease in quantity demanded, meaning that producers are more able to pass on most of the tax to consumers. Consumers pay to the extent of the price rise (from P to P'), this will be the greatest incidence of the tax. Any amount of the tax not covered by the price increase has to be absorbed by the firm (from P to A).

Inelastic demand

Taxes placed on goods that are price inelastic can raise significant revenue. The reason for this is that the price rise caused by the imposition of the tax on goods or services that are inelastic in nature will cause a proportionately small decrease in quantity demanded. This results in a relatively large number of goods or services on which the tax is imposed, and therefore greater tax revenue is collected. Given this, a government is more likely to impose taxes on products such as cigarettes and alcohol that are inelastic in nature, than products such as new cars.

The incidence of a tax falls more heavily on the producer when a good or service is elastic. When demand is elastic, a given increase in price will see a more than proportionate decrease in quantity demanded, meaning that producers are less able to pass the tax on to consumers. Consumers pay to the extent of the price increase that results from the tax. However, the greatest portion of the tax is not covered by the price increase and has to be absorbed by the firm.

Taxes placed on goods that are price elastic may raise less revenue than a tax placed on goods that are price inelastic. The reason for this is that the price rise caused by the imposition of the tax on goods or services that are elastic in nature will cause a proportionately large decrease in quantity demanded. This can leave only a relatively small number of goods or services on which the tax is imposed, and therefore less tax revenue is collected.

The incidence of a tax is dependent on the relative elasticities of demand and supply and can be seen on the two graphs.

When the demand curve is relatively elastic the producer is less able to pass on the tax to the consumer as shown in the diagram.

Elastic demand

QUESTIONS & TASKS

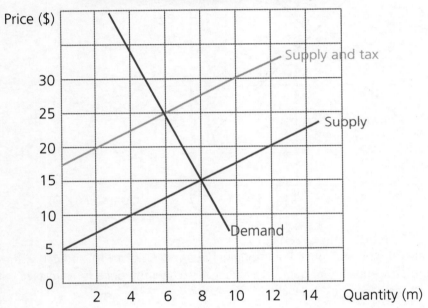

Sales tax and allocative efficiency

1 a Assume the government has placed a **per unit sales tax of $12**. On the graph above label:
- the original equilibrium price (Pe) and quantity (Qe)
- the new equilibrium price (Pc) and quantity (Qc)
- the new price producers receive as (Pp).

b Complete the table.

(i) Change in total consumer spending	
(ii) Change in suppliers' revenue	
(iii) Change in consumer surplus	
(iv) Change in producer surplus	
(v) Government revenue from the tax	
(vi) The deadweight loss	

2 Study the graph and answer the questions that follow.

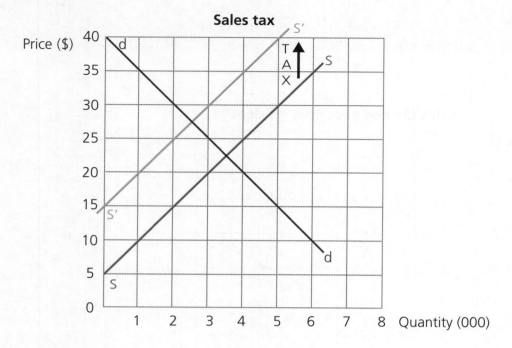

Sales tax

a On the above diagram label the original price P and original quantity Q. Label P1 and Q1 as the new equilibrium price and new equilibrium quantity respectively. Label the price firms receive with the sales tax as A.

b What is the value of the tax shown? _____

c Complete the table.

Question	Formula or letter	Value from graph
(i) Price paid by consumer before		
(ii) Price paid by consumer after		
(iii) Price firms receive after		
(iv) Value of sales before		
(v) Value of sales after		
(vi) Change in the value of sales		
(vii) Firms' revenue (income) after		
(viii) Change in the firms' revenue		
(ix) Tax revenue collected by government		
(x) Consumer surplus before		
(xi) Consumer surplus after		
(xii) Change in consumer surplus		
(xiii) Deadweight loss		

 ISBN: 9780170438117

3 Study the graph below and answer the questions that follow.

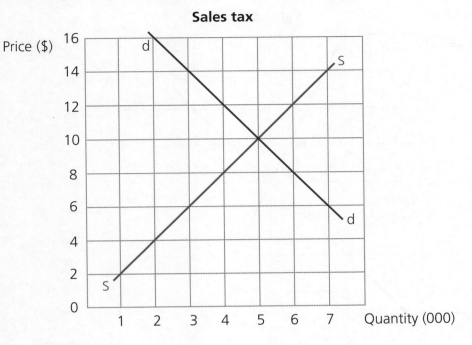

Sales tax

a Show on the above diagram a sales tax of $4 per item. Label the curve fully, showing the new price as P' and the new quantity as Q'. Label the new price firms receive as A.

b Calculate the change in consumer spending following the imposition of the sales tax. Show your working.

_____

_____

c What is the new equilibrium price? _____

d At the new equilibrium how much do firms earn per item? _____

e Calculate the change in firms' revenue following the imposition of the sales tax.

_____

_____

f Calculate the tax revenue collected by government. _____

g Consumers receive a certain amount of consumer surplus before and after a tax is imposed. Explain what the surplus represents.

_____

_____

_____

_____

_____

_____

_____

_____

4 Use the diagram to answer the questions in the table.

Sales tax

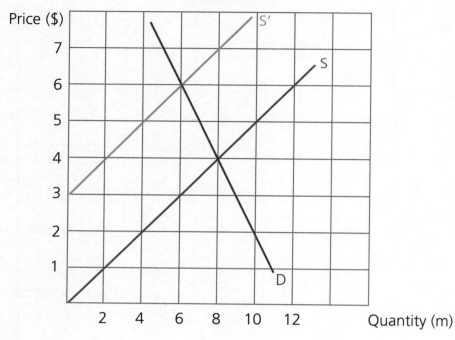

Question	Working and answer
a What price is paid by consumers before and after?	
b What is consumer expenditure before?	
c What is consumer expenditure after?	
d What is the change in consumer expenditure?	
e What is the government revenue from the tax?	
f Work out price elasticity of demand. | P ($)	Q
4	8m
6	6m		
g What is producer revenue before?	
h What is producer revenue after?	
i What is the change in producer revenue?	
j Work out the value of the deadweight loss.	
k What do the parallel lines on the diagram indicate?	
l Calculate PS before.	
m Calculate PS after.	
n Calculate the change in PS.	
o Calculate the change in CS.	

5 Study the diagram below and answer the questions that follow.

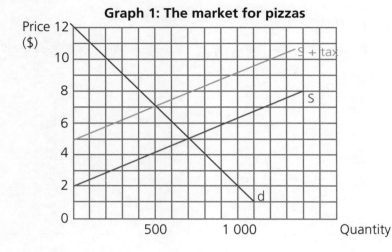

Graph 1: The market for pizzas

a Complete the table.

Question: Calculate	Working and answer
(i) CS before	
(ii) CS after	
(iii) Change in CS	
(iv) PS before	
(v) PS after	
(vi) Change in PS	

b (i) Calculate the tax per unit. _____

   (ii) Calculate the government revenue from the tax. _____

c Calculate:

   (i) the incidence of the sales tax on consumers (show your workings). _____

   (ii) the incidence of the sales tax on producers (show your workings). _____

d (i) How will the incidence of the sales tax change, the less price elastic the demand for pizzas becomes?

   _____

   _____

   _____

   (ii) Explain why the incidence of the sales tax will change.

   _____

   _____

   _____

e Shade the allocative efficiency that has been lost in the pizza market as a result of the sales tax being applied. Label this clearly.

6 The incidence of a tax is shared by buyers and sellers.

Fully explain the incidence of a tax. In your answer you should:

- Explain what is meant by the concept 'incidence of tax'.
- Explain, with the use of diagrams, how the incidence of tax is dependent on price elasticity of demand.

_____

_____

_____

_____

_____

_____

_____

_____

_____

_____

_____

_____

_____

_____

_____

_____

_____

_____

_____

_____

_____

_____

_____

_____

_____

_____

_____

_____

_____

7 Cigarette smokers will be hit hard by new tax.

Explain the effect of a $4.50 tax per unit on cigarettes. In your answer you should:

- State or calculate the missing values to questions (i) to (viii) in the table below.
- Explain why the demand for cigarettes is likely to be relatively price inelastic.
- Using the elasticity theory identify and explain the group that the incidence of the tax will fall more heavily on.
- Shade the deadweight loss resulting from the tax and explain why it occurs.

	Question	Answer
(i)	The new price consumers would pay per packet	
(ii)	The amount retailers will receive for themselves per packet	
(iii)	The new quantity sold per week	
(iv)	The tax revenue received by the government	
(v)	The change in total consumer spending	
(vi)	The change in suppliers' after-tax revenue	
(vii)	The producer surplus before the tax	
(viii)	The change in consumer surplus due to the tax	

_____

_____

_____

_____

_____

_____

_____

_____

_____

_____

_____

_____

_____

_____

_____

_____

10 EFFICIENCY OF MARKET EQUILIBRIUM
Subsidy and AE

Subsidy and allocative efficiency

A **subsidy** is a payment by government to firms to keep their costs down, and as a result firms will increase supply. As supply increases the equilibrium price will decrease and the equilibrium quantity will increase. To **illustrate the effects of a per unit (dollar) subsidy** requires shifting the original supply curve downward to the right by the per unit subsidy amount. For example, if the per unit subsidy is $5 and $5 equates to 5 spaces on the graph, you must shift the entire supply curve vertically downwards this distance. It is important to note that the decrease in the price will not be as much as the amount of the subsidy because the curves are sloping. In most cases part of the subsidy will benefit the consumer and part will benefit the firm.

Consumer Surplus

Producer Surplus

Subsidy

Deadweight Loss

Pe is the original price and Qe is the original quantity
P2 is the new price and Q2 is the new quantity
Pp is the price per item firms receive with a subsidy

	Original equilibrium	New equilibrium
Consumer surplus (CS)	0.5 × 4m × $8 = $16m	0.5 × 6m × $12 = $36m
Producer surplus (PS)	0.5 × 4m × $2 = $4m	0.5 × 6m × $3 = $9m
Deadweight loss (DWL)	Nil (zero)	0.5 × 2m x $5 = $5m

With a subsidy, consumer surplus will increase because consumers pay less and buy more. Producer surplus will increase because producers receive a higher price and sell more. There is a deadweight loss from the subsidy that represents the loss of allocative efficiency because part of the original consumer surplus and producer surplus is not picked up as part of the subsidy.

The impact of a subsidy worked example

	Before the subsidy	After the subsidy
Quantity sold	Qe, 4m	Q2, 6m
Price consumers pay	Pe, $8	P2, $4
Consumer spending	Pe x Qe, $32m	P2 x Q2, $24m
Price producers receive	Pe, $8	Pp, $9
Producer revenue	Pe x Qe, $32m	Pp x Q2, $54m
Change in the value of sales	(Pe x Qe) difference (P2 x Q2). A decrease of $8m	
Change in producers' revenue	(Pe x Qe) difference (Pp x Q2). An increase of $22m	
How much is the subsidy per unit?	The size of the gap between the supply curves. $5	
Cost to the government of the subsidy	Subsidy per unit x Q2. $5 x 6m = $30m	

The subsidy per unit is the gap between the supply curves. Note the price does not fall by the full amount of the subsidy per unit. In this case the subsidy per unit is $5 but the price has gone down by $4.

The **incidence of a subsidy** is a reference to who actually benefits from the government paying a subsidy. **Consumers** benefit to the extent of the price decreases from the original price paid (Pe) to the new price they pay (P2). Any amount of the subsidy not covered by the price decrease to consumers goes to the firm (from Pp to P2 on the diagram opposite).

The change in the value of consumer spending that results from the subsidy equals the difference between the original price a consumer pays (Pe) multiplied by the original quantity purchased (Qe) and the new price paid (P2) multiplied by the new quantity purchased (Q2). Since a subsidy results in a price decrease there will be an increase in quantity demanded because more consumers are more willing and able to purchase the good or service with their limited incomes.

The value of consumer spending may remain unchanged, decrease or increase because the new value of consumer spending depends on the relative changes in both the new price paid and the new quantity purchased. Consumers may look to buy a complement to use in conjunction with the subsidied good or service. Consumers may also look to buy less of a substitute good or service that is relatively more expensive.

Producers will find that the subsidy reduces their costs so they will increase supply, meaning that there will be an increase in quantity supplied at each and every price. The price per item that firms receive with a subsidy will be higher than the price that consumers pay them. To identify how much producers earn per item for the product you track up from the new equilibrium position until you hit the original supply curve, this gives the price per item firms receive with a subsidy (shown on the diagram as the letter Pp).

The change in the firm's income or revenue will be the difference between the firm's original income, which was the original price (Pe) received, multiplied by the original quantity (Qe) and the new value of the firm's income, which equals the price per item the firm now receives (Pp) multiplied by the new quantity sold (Q2). The producer's total income with the subsidy will increase because the price per item that the firm receives will be higher and the quantity sold will increase.

The cost to the **government** of the subsidy equals the subsidy per unit multiplied by the new quantity (subsidy per unit x Q2).

Incidence of a subsidy

Interpreting the graph	Letter answer
Total cost to government of the subsidy	B P' E A
Gain consumer surplus from the subsidy	P P' E C increase
Gain producer surplus from the subsidy	B P C A increase
Total deadweight loss	A C E

The incidence of a subsidy falls mainly on consumers when a good or service is inelastic. When demand is inelastic, a given decrease in price will see a less than proportionate increase in quantity demanded. It will result in a relatively large decrease in price paid by the consumer, with a relatively small increase in the quantity sold, therefore consumers rather than producers gain the most from the subsidy. Consumers benefit to the extent of the price decrease (from P to P'), which will be the greatest incidence of the subsidy. Any amount of the subsidy not covered by the price decrease will benefit the firm (from P to B).

The incidence of a subsidy falls more heavily on the producer when a good or service is elastic. When demand is elastic, a given decrease in price will see a more than proportionate increase in quantity demanded. It will result in a relatively small decrease in price paid by the consumer, with a relatively large increase in the quantity sold, therefore producers rather than consumers gain the most from the subsidy.

When demand is inelastic consumers benefit more (as shown in the left hand diagram) and when demand is elastic the incidence benefits the producer or seller more (as shown in right hand diagram).

That part of the subsidy paid by the government that does not form part of the new producer surplus or new consumer surplus is termed the deadweight loss (DWL). The DWL of a subsidy is shown as an inwardly pointed triangle (ACE).

QUESTIONS & TASKS

Subsidy and allocative efficiency

1 **a** Assume the government has placed a **per unit subsidy of $12**. On the graph above label:
  • the original equilibrium price (Pe) and quantity (Qe)
  • the new equilibrium price (Pc) and quantity (Qc)
  • the new price producers receive as (Pp).

b Complete the table.

(i) Change in total consumer spending	
(ii) Change in suppliers' revenue	
(iii) Change in consumer surplus	
(iv) Change in producer surplus	
(v) Cost to the government of the subsidy	
(vi) The deadweight loss	

2 Study the graph and answer the questions that follow.

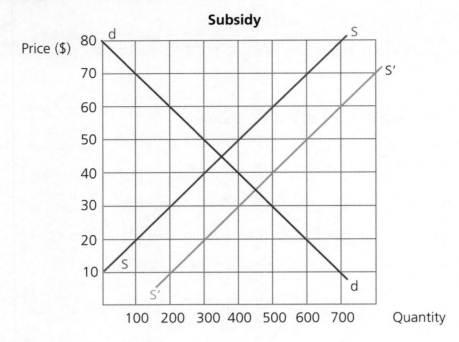

Subsidy

a On the above diagram label the original price P and new price P'. Label the original quantity Q and new quantity Q'. Label the price firms receive with a subsidy as B.

b What is the value of the subsidy shown per unit? _____

c Complete the table below.

Question	Formula or letter	Value from graph
(i) Value of sales before		
(ii) Value of sales after		
(iii) Change in the value of sales		
(iv) Firms' revenue before		
(v) Firms' revenue after		
(vi) Change in firms' revenue		
(vii) Price per item received by firms with subsidy		
(viii) Cost to government of the subsidy		
(ix) Consumer surplus before	½ x b x h	
(x) Consumer surplus after	½ x b' x h'	
(xi) Change in consumer surplus (CS)	(½ x b x h) vs (½ x b' x h')	
(xii) Total deadweight loss	½ x b x h	

3 a Use the diagram to answer the questions that follow in the table. Label the diagram appropriately.

Subsidy diagram

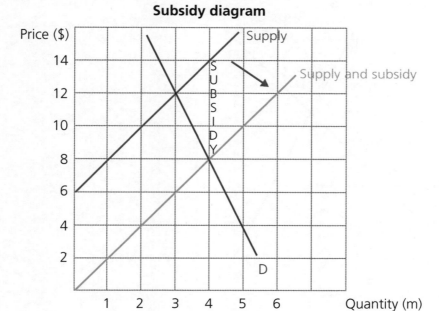

b What do the parallel lines on the diagram indicate? _____

c Shade in the area of the cost to the government of the subsidy.

Give the value to represent the following	Working and answer
(i) Price paid by consumer before	
(ii) Price paid by consumer after	
(iii) Consumer spending before	
(iv) Consumer spending after	
(v) Change in consumer surplus	
(vi) Change in producer surplus	
(vii) Cost to government of the subsidy	
(viii) Deadweight loss of the subsidy	

d Explain whether consumers or producers would receive the greater benefit of the subsidy. Use data in your answer.

_____

_____

_____

_____

_____

_____

4 Study the diagram below and answer the questions that follow.

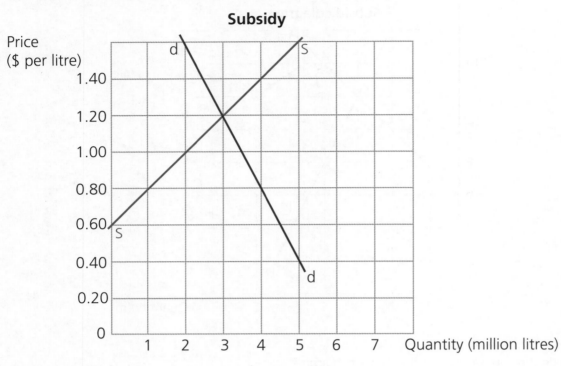

Subsidy

a Draw and label a new supply curve to show a subsidy of $0.60 per litre on the above diagram. Identify the new price paid by consumers as P' and price received by producers as B.

b Work out the new equilibrium price and quantity. _____

c Work out the change in the value of sales.

_____

d At the new equilibrium how much do firms earn per item? _____

e Calculate the change in firms' income.

_____

f Calculate the cost to the government of the subsidy. _____

g **(i)** Explain, with reference to the diagram, who benefits more from the subsidy, consumers or producers.

_____

_____

_____

   (ii) Shade in consumer and producer incidence of the subsidy. Label clearly.

   (iii) Calculate the change in CS. _____

   (iv) Calculate the change in PS. _____

5 Study the diagram and answer the questions that follow.

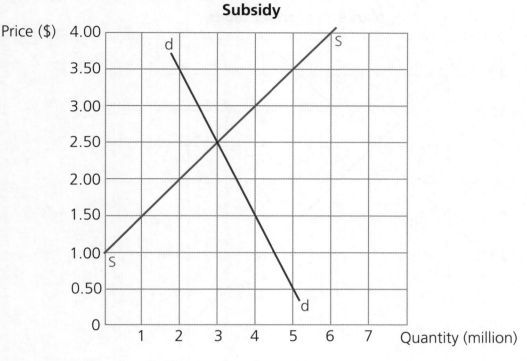

Subsidy

a What is the original:

(i) equilibrium price? _____   **(iii)** value of sales? _____

(ii) equilibrium quantity? _____   **(iv)** firms' income? _____

b (i) Assume the government gives $1.50 subsidy on each item. Draw and label the new curve on the graph.

(ii) What is the new equilibrium price and quantity?

price _____ quantity _____

(iii) What is the value of sales now? _____

(iv) At the new equilibrium how much do firms earn per item? _____

(v) At the new equilibrium what is the firms' revenue? _____

(vi) Calculate the cost of the subsidy to the government. _____

(vii) Calculate the change in consumer surplus. _____

c (i) Define allocative efficiency.

_____

_____

_____

(ii) Shade in the deadweight loss resulting from the subsidy and explain why this deadweight loss occurs.

_____

_____

_____

6 Study the graph 'Market for school shoes' and answer the questions that follow.

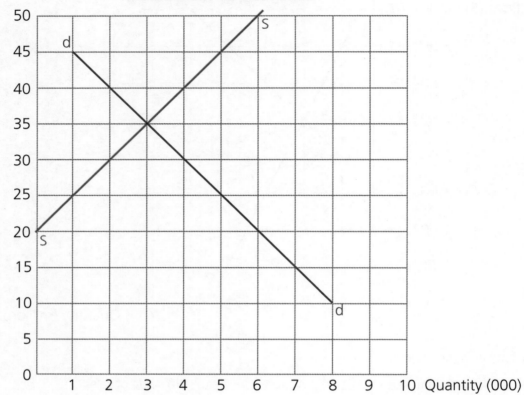

Market for school shoes

Price ($ per pair of shoes)

Quantity (000)

a (i) How much would the subsidy have to be per pair of shoes for the price to fall to $25?

_____

(ii) On the diagram show the effect of a subsidy that results in a price of $25 per pair of shoes. Label the new equilibrium quantity Q'.

b (i) What price does the producer receive after the subsidy?

_____

(ii) What is total consumer spending after the subsidy? _____

(iii) Calculate the cost to the government of such a subsidy. _____

(iv) Calculate the change in consumer surplus.

_____

(v) Calculate the change in producer surplus.

_____

(vi) Calculate the deadweight loss.

_____

ISBN: 9780170438117

7 A subsidy will have different consequences for consumers, producers and government.

Explain the consequences of a subsidy on various groups. In your answer you should use data from the graph and:

- Explain the consequences of the subsidy on consumers.
- Explain the consequences of the subsidy on producers.
- Explain the consequences on government of the subsidy and the loss of allocative efficiency.

Bus trips per year

_____

_____

_____

_____

_____

_____

_____

_____

_____

_____

_____

_____

_____

_____

_____

_____

11 EFFICIENCY OF MARKET EQUILIBRIUM
Maximum price and AE

Maximum price control and allocative efficiency

A **price control** (maximum or minimum price) is imposed by government so that price cannot automatically move back to the equilibrium as it would in the free market because laws or regulations prohibit this.

A **maximum price** (or **ceiling price**) is a price control set by government prohibiting the charging of a price higher than a certain level. A maximum price is set in the interests of consumers to protect them from paying unreasonably high prices for essential goods and services, for example housing, petrol or certain food items such as bread and milk.

To illustrate the effects of a maximum price, draw a line at the price at which the maximum price is set and label this appropriately. Draw a dotted line to show the quantity demanded (Qd) and quantity supplied (Qs) at this price, than label the resulting shortage created. Show the decrease in price from the original price (Pe) to the maximum price (Pmax)

Market for bread and a maximum price

Pe is the original price and Qe is the original quantity

Qd is the new quantity demanded by consumers after the maximum price (Pmax)

Qs is the new quantity supplied by producers after the maximum price (Pmax)

	Original equilibrium	New equilibrium
Consumer surplus (CS)	0.5 × 8m × $2 = $8m	(0.5 × 4m × $1) plus (4m x $2) = $10m
Producer surplus (PS)	0.5 × 8m × $2 = $8m	(0.5 × 4m × $1) = $2m
Deadweight loss (DWL)	Nil (zero)	0.5 × 4m × $2 = $4m

There is a deadweight loss from a maximum price that represents the loss of allocative efficiency because part of the original consumer surplus and producer surplus is not picked up as part of the maximum price.

       ISBN: 9780170438117

The impact of a maximum price worked example

	Before the maximum price	After the maximum price
Quantity sold	Qe, 8m	Q2, 4m
Price consumers pay	Pe, $3	Pmax, $2
Consumer spending	Pe x Qe, 24m	Pmax x Q2, $8m
Price producers receive	Pe, $3	Pmax, $2
Producer revenue	Pe x Qe, $24m	Pmax x Q2, $8m
Size of the shortage	The size of the gap between Q2 and Qd. 8m	

If the government sets a maximum price control of $2 for the market of bread this restricts the price that firms are legally allowed to charge. The diagram shows that imposing a maximum price at $2 for a loaf of bread will cause the price to fall from $3 to $2. As the price decreases the quantity demanded of bread made available by producers decreases from 8m (Qe) to 4m (Qs). This causes a shortage of 8m loaves of bread and could give rise to a black market where some people are willing to pay a higher price than the legally set price by government of $2 for bread.

The change in total value of sales after the maximum price is imposed is the difference between the original price multiplied by the original quantity (Pe multiplied by Qe) and the maximum price set multiplied by the quantity made available by suppliers (Maximum Price multiplied by Qs). In this instance, it is the difference between ($3 multiplied by 8m) and ($2 multiplied by 4m) which is a $16m decrease.

To assist individuals and families to buy affordable bread to eat the government could increase the supply of bread by offering producers a subsidy. A subsidy is a payment by government to suppliers (businesses) to keep costs down, as a result they will increase supply and the price will decrease. The advantage of a subsidy over a maximum price control is that there will be no shortage and the market will clear. The disadvantage of a subsidy is that it may be very expensive for the government, and the money spent on the subsidised good or service means this money cannot be spent elsewhere.

A maximum price set above the equilibrium price has no effect because a price above the equilibrium price creates a surplus (excess supply) where market forces automatically cause the price to decrease back to the equilibrium. Therefore, to be effective, a maximum price must be set below the equilibrium.

The **advantages of a maximum price** control is that it will lower the price of the good or service and make it more affordable for consumers, and there is no cost to the government. The problem of an effective maximum price set below the equilibrium is that it distorts the market because it does not allow the market to clear. A maximum price set below the equilibrium results in a shortage (excess demand), because at prices below the equilibrium the quantity demanded by consumers is greater than the quantity supplied by producers. This means that some consumers who had the good or service before the maximum price was imposed miss out because the quantity supplied decreases as the price falls. Solutions to overcome the shortage created by a maximum price could be first-come-first-served until supply runs out, or the government could issue ration cards giving an equal share to everyone.

A **black market** can arise with a maximum price. A black market is part of the underground or informal economy where activities that take place are illegal, unregulated and not taxed. In a black market, firms charge a price above the legally set government maximum price or well-off customers or consumers pay more than the government's legally set price to obtain the good or service that circumvents rationing measures put in place by the government.

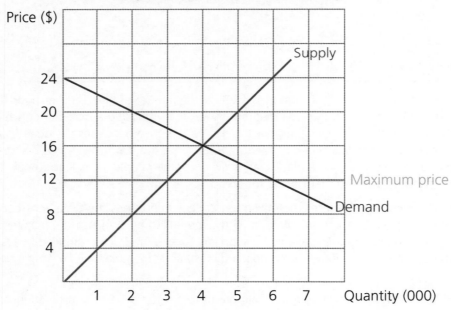

Maximum price and allocative efficiency

1 **a** Assume the government has placed a **maximum price control of $12**.
      On the graph above label:
      • the original equilibrium price (Pe) and quantity (Qe)
      • the new equilibrium price (Pc) and quantity (Qc)
      • the new price producers receive as (Pp).

   b Complete the table.

(i) Change in total consumer spending	
(ii) Change in consumer surplus	
(iii) Change in producer surplus	
(iv) The deadweight loss	

2 a Show the effects of a maximum price of $3.20 per litre on the graph below (labelled as Pmax) on the market for milk each month.

Market for milk each month

Price ($ per litre)

Quantity (million litres)

b Referring to the graph, identify:

- the price that consumers pay before and after: before: _____

  after: _____

- the price that producers receive before and after: before: _____

  after: _____

- the value of sales before and after: before: _____

  after: _____

c Discuss the effect on consumer spending and consumers of the maximum price.

_____

_____

_____

_____

_____

_____

_____

_____

_____

_____

_____

_____

_____

3 Use the diagram below to answer the questions that follow.

Market for houses for rent

The government wants to reduce the cost of houses for rent. One option is to impose a price control of $175.

a What is the correct economic term for this option? _____

b **(i)** Show the effect on the graph of the government imposing a price control of $175.

(ii) Calculate the change in producer surplus from the maximum price. Shade and label this area.

_____

_____

c Alternatively, the government could achieve the same market price of $175 by offering a subsidy. How much would the subsidy on each house have to be?

_____

d Calculate the cost of the subsidy to the government.

_____

e Both price control and subsidy options achieve the same market price but have different effects on the quantity supplied. For each option calculate the change in quantity supplied.

(i) price control option _____ **(ii)** subsidy option _____

f State one advantage of subsidies over price controls.

_____

_____

   ISBN: 9780170438117

4 Price controls can cause the market to be allocatively inefficient.

Explain the effects of a price control. In your answer you should use the graph and:

- Label the original equilibrium price and quantity as Pe and Qe respectively. Calculate the original value of CS and PS.
- Label the new equilibrium price and quantity as P1 and Q1 respectively. Calculate the new CS and PS after the increase in demand.
- Explain how the market restores the equilibrium.
- Assume the government fixes the price at Pe, shade the deadweight loss and explain why it occurs.

Market for smoke alarms

_____

_____

_____

_____

_____

_____

_____

_____

_____

_____

_____

_____

_____

_____

_____

_____

_____

_____

_____

Minimum price control and allocative efficency

A **minimum price** (or **floor price**) is a price control set by government where the market price is not allowed to fall below a certain minimum (floor) level. A minimum price is set by the government in the interests of producers to protect them from volatile prices in world markets and ensure that they are not receiving an unreasonably low price for what they produce. At one time in New Zealand, the government set a minimum (floor) price on wool and butter.

To illustrate the effects of a minimum price, draw a line at the price at which the minimum price is set and label this appropriately. Draw a dotted line to show the quantity demanded (Qd) and quantity supplied (Qs) at this price, than label the resulting surplus created. Show the increase in price from the original price (Pe) to the minimum price (Pmin)

Market for wool and a minimum price

Pe is the original price and Qe is the original quantity

Qd is the new quantity demanded by consumers after the minimum price (Pmin)

Qs is the new quantity supplied by producers after the minimum price (Pmin)

	Original equilibrium	New equilibrium
Consumer surplus (CS)	(0.5 × 8m × $8) = $32m	(0.5 × 4m × $4) = $8m
Producer surplus (PS)	(0.5 × 8m × $4) = $16m	(4m × $6 plus 0.5 × 4m x $2) = $28m
Deadweight loss (DWL)	Nil (zero)	0.5 × 4m x $6 = $12m

There is a deadweight loss from a minimum price that represents the loss of allocative efficiency because part of the original consumer surplus and producer surplus is not picked up as part of the miniimum price.

The impact of a minimum price worked example

	Before the minimum price	After the minimum price
Quantity sold	Qe, 8 million	Qd, 4 million
Price consumers pay	Pe, $10	Pmin, $14
Consumer spending	Pe x Qe, $80m	Pe x Qd, $56m
Price producers receive	Pe, $10	Pmin, $14
Size of the surplus	The size of the gap between Qd and Qs. 12 million	

If the government sets a minimum price control of $14 on the market for wool, the diagram shows, the price of wool will increase from $10 to $14. As the price increases the quantity of wool demanded by consumers decreases from 8 million (Qe) to 4 million (Qd). There is a surplus of 12 million that the government has to buy and store.

The change in total value of sales after the minimum price is imposed is the difference between the original price multiplied by the original quantity (Pe multiplied by Qe) and the minimum price set multiplied by the quantity purchased by consumers (Minimum Price multiplied by Qd). In this instance, it is a $24m decrease.

The change in a firms revenue is the difference between the original price multiplied by the original quantity (Pe multiplied by Qe) and the minimum price set multiplied by the quantity produced by producers (Minimum Price multiplied by Qs) if the government purchases the excess supply of wool. Left to the free operation of the market this surplus goes unsold and creates a deadweight loss.

To be effective, a minimum price is set above the equilibrium price. This encourages producers to increase the quantity supplied because they are more able to cover their costs because they are earning higher revenue and it is more profitable to produce the good or service. The problem of an effective minimum price set above the equilibrium is that it distorts the market because it does not allow the market to clear. At the higher price the quantity demanded by consumers is less than the quantity supplied by producers resulting in excess supply (a surplus). The surplus (excess supply) is created because price is not allowed to fall below the controlled price to the equilibrium. The government then has to decide what to do with the surplus stock. In the past this surplus stock was stockpiled and sold at a later date.

A minimum price set below the equilibrium price has no effect because a price below the equilibrium price creates a shortage (excess demand) where market forces automatically cause price to increase back to the equilibrium. Therefore, to be effective, a minimum price must be set above the equilibrium.

QUESTIONS & TASKS

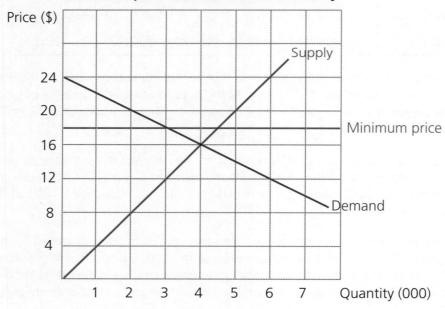

Minimum price and allocative efficiency

1 **a** Assume the government has placed a **minimum price control of $18**.
On the graph above label:
  • the original equilibrium price (Pe) and quantity (Qe)
  • the new equilibrium price (Pc) and quantity (Qc)
  • the new price producers receive as (Pp).

b Complete the table.

(i) Change in total consumer spending	
(ii) Change in consumer surplus	
(iii) Change in producer surplus	
(iv) The deadweight loss	

       ISBN: 9780170438117

Market for kiwifruit annually

Price $ per kg (vertical axis): 1–8

Quantity (million kg) (horizontal axis): 2–18

S — supply curve
D — demand curve

2 a Show a minimum price of kiwifruit set at $5 per kg.

b Referring to the graph above, identify and calculate:

	Before the minimum price	After the minimum price
Quantity sold		
Price consumers pay		
Consumer spending		
Size of the surplus		

c Referring to the graph above, identify and calculate:

	Before the minimum price	After the minimum price
Consumer surplus		
Producer surplus		
Change in CS		
Change in PS		
Deadweight loss		

Prices for avocados continue to vary.

3 The graph shows the effects of a minimum price on the market for avocados.

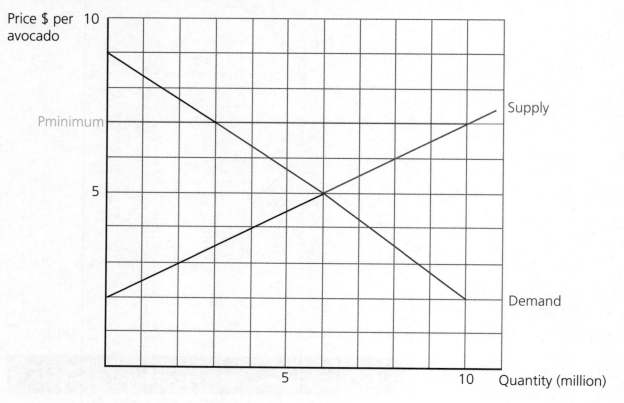

Price $ per avocado

Pminimum

Supply

Demand

Quantity (million)

a On the graph above:

(i) use dotted lines to show the original equilibrium price and quantity (label as **Pe** and **Qe**)

(ii) use dotted lines to show the new quantity demanded (**Qd**) and supplied (**Qs**)

(iii) label the resulting **surplus** or **shortage**.

b Referring to the graph above, identify and calculate:

	Before the price control	After the price control
(i) Consumer spending		
(ii) Consumer surplus		
(iii) Producer surplus		
(iv) Deadweight loss		

4 a Show the effects of a minimum price of $12 per kg on the graph below (labelled as Pmin) on the market for cheese each month. Shade and label the new consumer surplus **(i)**, producer surplus **(ii)** and any loss of allocative efficiency **(iii)**.

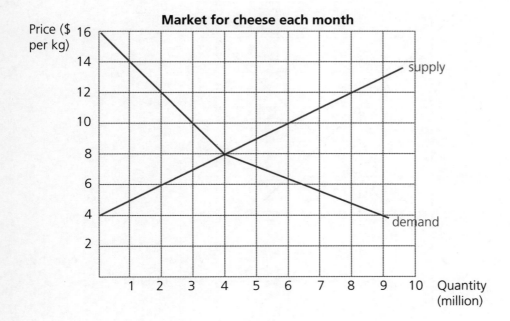

Market for cheese each month

b What difficulty does the government face with getting a price control of $12 per kg?

_____

_____

_____

_____

_____

c Why might a government impose a minimum price?

_____

_____

_____

5 a On the graph of the Weekly market for organic eggs below, show the effect of a minimum price of $7 per dozen (labelled as Pmin).

Weekly market for organic eggs

Price ($ per dozen) / Quantity (000) dozen

b Referring to the graph, identify:

- the price that consumers pay before and after the minimum price

  before: _____   after: _____

- the price that producers receive before and after the minimum price

  before: _____   after: _____

- the quantity that consumers buy before and after the minimum price

  before: _____   after: _____

c Referring to the graph, calculate the values before and after the minimum price.

	Before the minimum price	After the minimum price
Consumer surplus		
Producer surplus		
Deadweight loss		

Market for lambs

Price ($)

6 **a** The government has imposed a minimum price of $180 per lamb. Label at the minimum price
   Consumer surplus
   Producer surplus
   Deadweight loss (if any)

b Complete the table

	Value from the graph
(i) Change in consumer surplus	
(ii) Original producer surplus	
(iii) New producer surplus	
(iv) Change in producer surplus	
(iv) Deadweight loss	

13 EFFICIENCY OF MARKET EQUILIBRIUM
Free trade and AE

Free trade is trade between countries without government intervention. Changes that take place in the market as a result of free trade allow the market to reach the equilibrium and the consumer surplus and producer surplus are still maximised. International free trade is more allocatively efficient than not trading, because the area of total surpluses increases.

Free trade – exports (X)

Pe is the original price and Qe is the original quantity. Pw is the new price and Qd is the new quantity. The gap between Qd and Qs represents exports (X).

	Original equilibrium	New equilibrium
Consumer surplus (CS)	0.5 × 6m × $8 = $24m	0.5 × 3m × $4 = $6m
Producer surplus (PS)	0.5 × 6m × $4 = $12m	0.5 × 12m x $8 = $48m
Deadweight loss (DWL)	Nil (zero)	Nil (zero)

With the free trade in eggs the increase in producer surplus of $36m offsets the decrease in consumer surplus of $18m. The market is allocatively efficient because the total surpluses increase by $18m.

The diagram shows that with free trade the price that consumers pay for eggs increases from Pe ($6 per dozen) to Pw ($10 per dozen). As the price increases the quantity demanded of eggs by local consumers decreases from Qe (6 million dozen) to Qd (3 million dozen). The value of sales to local consumers decreases from $36m to $30m. Consumer surplus decreases because consumers pay more and buy fewer eggs.

The producer now receives Pw ($10 per dozen) rather than Pe ($6 per dozen). They now sell 3m dozen eggs to local consumers and export 9m dozen eggs to overseas buyers. The revenue for the producer will increase from $36m to $120m, of which $30m comes from domestic sales and $90m from export sales. Producer surplus increases because producers receive a higher price and sell more eggs.

Free trade – imports (M)

Market for books (free trade – CS/PS)

Consumer surplus ▬

Producer surplus ▬

Pe2 is the original price and Qe2 is the original quantity

Pw2 is the new price and Qd is the new quantity

The gap between Qs and Qd is the quantity of imports (M)

	Original equilibrium	New equilibrium
Consumer surplus (CS)	0.5 × 4m × $30 = $60m	0.5 × 6m × $45 = $135m
Producer surplus (PS)	0.5 × 4m × $30 = $60m	0.5 × 2m x $15 = $15m
Deadweight loss (DWL)	Nil (zero)	Nil (zero)

Overall net welfare increases because the decrease in producer surplus of $45m is more than offset by the gain in consumer surplus of $75m.

The diagram shows that the price that consumers pay for books decreases from Pe2 ($40) to Pw2 ($25). As the price decreases the quantity demanded of books by local consumers increases from Qe2 (4 million) to Qd (6 million). The value of sales decreases from $160m to $150m. Consumer surplus increases because they pay less and buy more.

Local producers have to lower the price to compete with cheaper imported books. They now receive Pw2 ($25) per book rather than Pe2 ($40), selling 2m books (Qs) rather than 4 million books. Their revenue will decrease from $160m to $50m. There is $100m spent on imported books because 4 million books are imported and sold at $25 per copy. Producer surplus decreases because they receive a lower price and sell less.

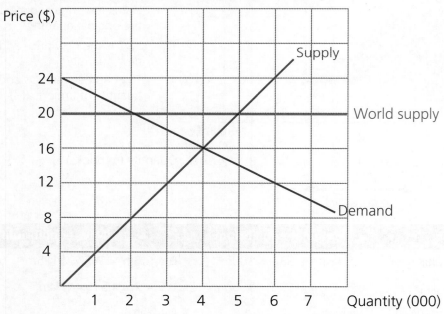

Free trade and allocative efficiency

1 a Assume **free trade** is taking place at a price of **$20**.
On the graph above label:
- the original equilibrium price (Pe) and quantity (Qe)
- the new equilibrium price (Pc) and quantity (Qc).

b Complete the table.

(i) Change in total consumer spending	
(ii) Change in suppliers' revenue	
(iii) Change in consumer surplus	
(iv) Change in producer surplus	
(v) The deadweight loss	

2 Study the diagram below and answer the questions that follow.

Trade diagram – New Zealand domestic market for milk weekly

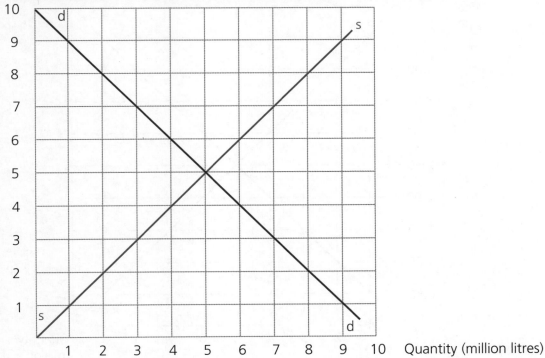

Price ($) per litre

Quantity (million litres)

a If the world price was $7, identify on the graph: **(i)** the quantity supplied and label it Qs.
(ii) the quantity demanded and label it Qd.   **(iii)** the quantity exported or imported.

b Calculate at the world price:

(i) the change in the total value of sales to the local market.

_____

(ii) the quantity of milk exported. _____

(iii) State the total revenue at the world price of $7. Show your working. _____

(iv) How much revenue is from domestic sales? _____

(v) How much revenue is from export sales? _____

c Calculate:

(i) CS before _____   **(iv)** PS before _____

(ii) CS after _____   **(v)** PS after _____

(iii) Change in CS _____   **(vi)** Change in PS _____

d Shade in the loss of consumer surplus.

3 Study the graph and answer the questions that follow.

New Zealand market for cheese

a What is a quota? How does a quota on New Zealand cheese to Europe and the USA affect New Zealand cheese production?

_____

_____

b The world price for cheese is above the market equilibrium price and is the same for all levels of quantity.

(i) Draw the world price at $3.50 per kg and label it P_W.

(ii) What happens to the New Zealand market price if New Zealand is involved in the trade of cheese with other countries? Be specific. _____

(iii) At a price of $3.50 per kg the New Zealand market has a surplus or excess supply. What will happen to this surplus? _____

(iv) Identify the new quantity of cheese sold in New Zealand at the world price. _____

(v) Calculate the decrease in the quantity sold in New Zealand. _____

(vi) Calculate the quantity of exports at the new world price. _____

c Shade in and label the change in producer surplus.

      ISBN: 9780170438117

4 The world price for snapper is above the market equilibrium in New Zealand.

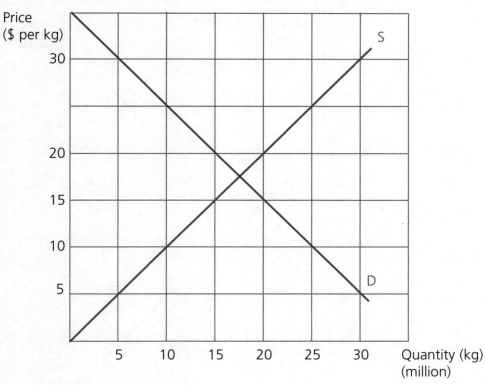

a Draw the world price at $25 per kg and label it P_W on the diagram above.

b What happens to the New Zealand domestic market price if New Zealand is involved in the trade of snapper?

_____

c At a price of $25 per kg the New Zealand market has a surplus. What will happen to this surplus?

_____

d Identify the new quantity demanded in New Zealand at $25 per kg as Qd′.

_____

e **(i)** State the total revenue at the world price of $25 per kg. Show your working.

_____

(ii) How much revenue is from:

domestic sales _____

export sales _____

f Explain why international trade in snapper is allocatively more efficient for New Zealand than not trading.

_____

_____

_____

_____

_____

5 Study the graph below and answer the questions that follow.

Trade diagram

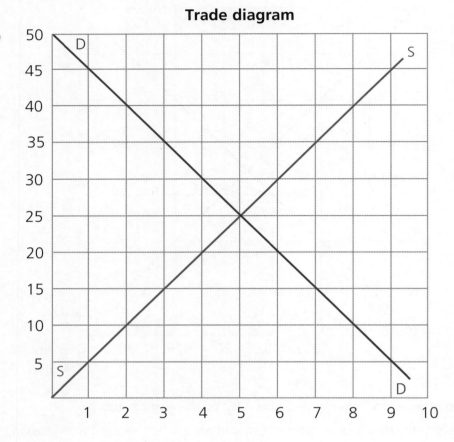

Price ($)

Quantity (000)

a If the world price is $15 and there were no trade restrictions, what would happen to the New Zealand domestic price? Explain why this would happen.

_____

_____

b (i) Draw on the diagram above a world price of $15 and label it P$_W$.

(ii) What is the new equilibrium price? _____

(iii) By what quantity has the sale of the product in New Zealand changed?

_____

(iv) How many of the product do New Zealand firms supply to the market at the new price?

_____

(v) Calculate the change in revenue for local (New Zealand) producers. Show your working.

_____

c Calculate:

(i) CS before _____ **(iv)** PS before _____

(ii) CS after _____ **(v)** PS after _____

(iii) Change in CS _____ **(vi)** Change in PS _____

d Show and clearly label on the diagram above the change in consumer surplus that results from the world price of $15.

6 Assume New Zealand is a price taker in the market for mountain bikes and the current world price expressed in NZ dollars is $1 500.

Explain the impact of trade in the market. In your answer you should:

- Show on Graph 1 the world price for mountain bikes, label it Pw, the quantity of mountain bikes imported, label it M, and the increase in consumer surplus as a result of international trade in mountain bikes, shade it.
- Explain why international trade in mountain bikes is allocatively more efficient for New Zealand than not trading.

Graph 1: Market for mountain bikes in New Zealand

_____

_____

_____

_____

_____

_____

_____

_____

_____

_____

_____

_____

_____

_____

_____

_____

_____

_____

_____

7 The removal of trade barriers will improve allocative efficiency.

Explain how removing a trade barrier is allocatively efficient. In your answer you should use the diagram drawn and:

- Explain why the world supply curve is drawn as a horizontal line.
- Identify clearly areas of CS and PS before and after trade barriers are removed.
- Explain the effect of free trade on New Zealand consumers, producers and the allocation of labour resources.

Domestic market in New Zealand for bacon

_____

_____

_____

_____

_____

_____

_____

_____

_____

_____

_____

_____

_____

_____

_____

_____

_____

_____

_____

8 Exporters expect to benefit from free trade deals being signed, but consumers will lose.

Explain how removing a trade barrier is allocatively efficient. In your answer you should use the diagram drawn and:

Explain how exporters gain from a free trade deal. In your answer you should:

- Draw a sketch diagram to show changes in CS and PS as a result of exporting.
- Explain the effect of exporting on consumers and producers.
- Explain the possible effects of exporting on government revenue.

_____

_____

_____

_____

_____

_____

_____

_____

_____

_____

_____

_____

_____

_____

_____

_____

_____

_____

_____

_____

_____

_____

_____

_____

_____

_____

_____

14 EFFICIENCY OF MARKET EQUILIBRIUM
Protectionism and AE

Protectionism refers to government measures (quotas and tariffs) that limit international trade. Protectionism will alter the market equilibrium in a way that results in a loss of allocative efficiency (termed deadweight loss).

Tariff & DWL

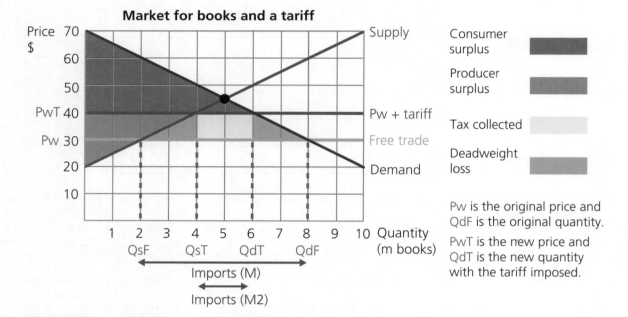

Market for books and a tariff

Pw is the original price and QdF is the original quantity.

PwT is the new price and QdT is the new quantity with the tariff imposed.

	Original equilibrium	New equilibrium
Consumer surplus (CS)	0.5 × 8m × $40 = $160m	0.5 × 6m × $30 = $90m
Producer surplus (PS)	0.5 × 2m × $10 = $10m	0.5 × 4m x $20 = $40m
Deadweight loss (DWL)	Nil (zero)	2 x (0.5 x 2m x $10) = $20m

With a per unit tariff of $10 placed on books, the equilibrium price increases from $30 (Pw) to $40 (PwT) and the equilibrium quantity decreases from 8m (QdF) to 6m (QdT). The quantity produced by local firms will now be 4m books (QsT) rather than 2m (QsF). The change in local firms' revenue is the difference between $60m ($30 x 2m books) and $160m ($40 x 4m books), which is an increase of $100m.

With the tariff in place, the quantity of books imported is now 2m books rather than the 6m previously imported when the price was $30. Part of the total value of consumer spending on books of $240m ($40 multiplied by 6m) will be $80m on imported books (imports multiplied by the world price), while the remaining $160m is with domestic (local) firms. The revenue received by the government is equal to the quantity imported multiplied by the per unit tariff imposed, (2m x $10), which is $20m.

There is a deadweight loss from the tariff that represents the loss of allocative efficiency because part of the original consumer surplus and producer surplus is not picked as part of the tariff imposed.

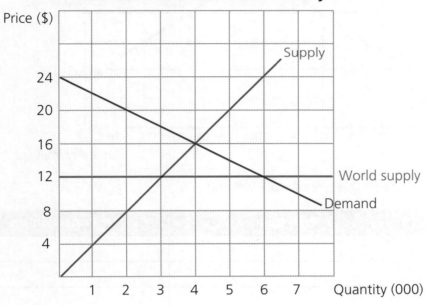

Protectionism and allocative efficiency

1 a On the graph above label the original free trade equilibrium price (Pe) and quantity (Qe)

b Assume that a **per unit tariff of $2 is imposed**. Draw and label the new supply curve.

Shade the gain in producer surplus ▰▰▰

Label the tax revenue collected ⊤⊤⊤⊤

Shade the loss of allocative efficiency ⠿⠿⠿

c Complete the table.

(i) Change in total consumer spending	
(ii) Change in suppliers' revenue	
(iii) Change in consumer surplus	
(iv) Change in producer surplus	
(v) The deadweight loss	

Graph: Trade – Protectionism

2 **a** Complete the table, using figures. Show your working.

	Free trade	Protectionism
Price		
Local firms' output		
Consumer expenditure		
Imports		
Consumer surplus		
Producer surplus		
Deadweight loss (DWL)		

b Explain why there is a change in consumer surplus and producer surplus.

_____

_____

_____

_____

_____

_____

_____

Protectionism/free trade

3 Study the diagram then use letters to complete the table below.

	Protectionism	Free trade
a Price		
b Local firms' output		
c Imports		
d Consumer surplus		
e Producer surplus		
f Deadweight loss (DWL)		

4 Explain, using figures, the changes to consumer surplus, producer surplus and allocative efficiency as the result of government imposing a per unit tariff of $15.

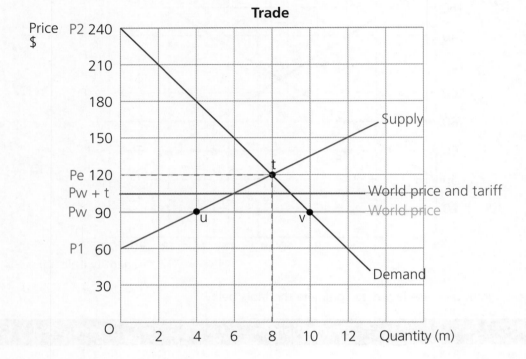

_____

_____

_____

_____

_____

_____

_____

_____

_____

_____

_____

_____

_____

_____

_____

_____

_____

_____

_____

5 Referring to the graph below, fully explain (using letters) the impact on consumers, producers, the government and allocative efficiency of a tariff imposed on this market.

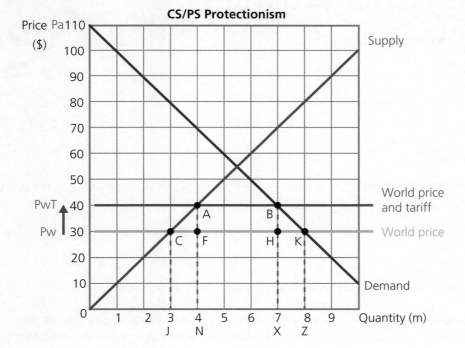

CS/PS Protectionism

_____
_____
_____
_____
_____
_____
_____
_____
_____
_____
_____
_____
_____
_____
_____
_____
_____
_____
_____
_____
_____
_____

15 REVISION/STUDY
Tasks and activities

Exam hints

Preparation

Prepare for the exam by completing all exericises in this book, doing old papers or the written questions on eLearneconomics.com website.

In the exam

- Use appropriate economic language, examples and terms in your answers.

- Make accurate references in your answers to the resource material and/or graphs drawn, i.e., provide details in your descriptions, such as figures or names of individuals/firms/products.

- Take care and construct well-labelled, accurate graphs (with a title, graduated scales) using a ruler to plot curves. Refer to these graphs explicitly in your explanations, e.g., D1 to D2, P to P'.

- Write structured answers that link ideas, keep your answers on track and do not contradict what you have written.

- Read questions carefully and add reasons, causes and effects in your explanations.

- Flow-on effects need to be valid, explained in full and kept in context with the event that led to it, rather than a restatement of the initial event itself.

- Attempt all questions.

- Present answers in a legible form.

- Use a pen (not a pencil) on your script to ensure answers are clear.

- Do not use abbreviations or text language because these are not appropriate in a formal exam.

       ISBN: 9780170438117

Notes

_____

_____

_____

_____

_____

_____

_____

_____

_____

_____

_____

_____

_____

_____

_____

_____

_____

_____

_____

_____

_____

_____

_____

_____

_____

_____

_____

_____

_____

_____

_____

_____

_____

_____

Question one: Maximum price

a Using market forces, explain how the market equilibrium is restored. Refer to the diagram in your answer.

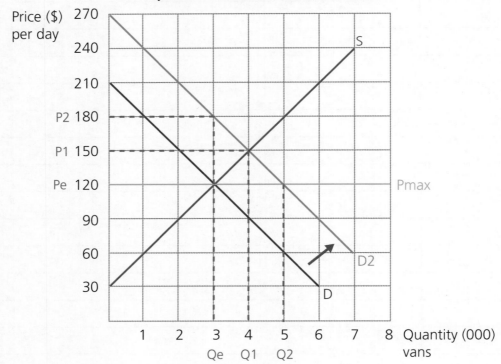

Campervan market in New Zealand

_____

_____

_____

_____

_____

_____

_____

_____

_____

_____

_____

_____

_____

_____

_____

_____

_____

_____

_____

b Compare and contrast the situation of the government leaving the market at the new equilibrium with the effect of imposing a maximum price of $120 per day on campervan rentals. Explain the impact on consumer surplus, producer surplus and allocative efficiency.

_____

_____

_____

_____

_____

_____

_____

_____

_____

_____

_____

_____

_____

_____

_____

_____

_____

_____

_____

_____

_____

_____

_____

_____

_____

_____

_____

_____

_____

_____

_____

_____

_____

_____

_____

_____

_____

Question two: A tariff

Study the diagram and answer the questions that follow.

Market for New Zealand clothes

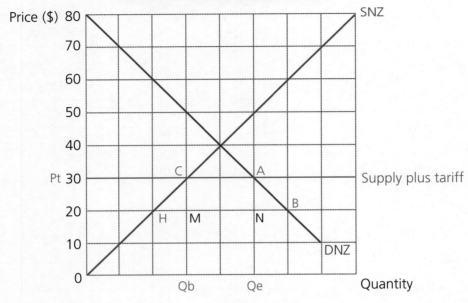

a Discuss the impact on allocative efficiency in the Market for New Zealand Clothes if the government removes the tariff on clothes. In your answer:

(i) Illustrate the removal of a per unit tariff of $10, label your new curve as Supply no tariff. Label the new equilibrium price as **Pf**, the new equilibrium quantity as **Qc**, local firms' output as **Qf** and the new level of imports as **M2**.

(ii) Explain in detail the changes made on your graph.

_____

_____

_____

_____

_____

_____

_____

_____

_____

_____

_____

_____

_____

_____

_____

_____

b Compare and contrast the impact of the government removing the tariff on consumers, producers, the government, and allocative efficiency. Refer to your diagram in your answer.

Question three: Sales tax and elasticity

Complete **a** and **b** to explain the impact of a sales tax on allocative efficiency in the market when goods or services are either price elastic or price inelastic.

Diagram 1: Elastic demand

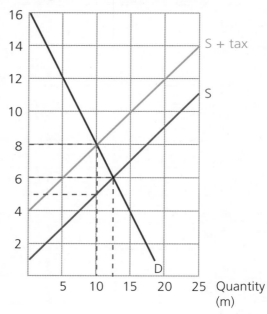

Diagram 2: Inelastic demand

a Complete the table below, use figures and show your working:

	Diagram 1	Diagram 2
(i) The new price		
(ii) The new quantity		
(iii) The change in consumer surplus		
(iv) The change in producer surplus		
(v) The deadweight loss		
(vi) The tax revenue for government		

b Compare and contrast the impact of a per unit sales tax on allocative efficiency when goods or services have different elasticities.

Explain the change in consumer surplus, producer surplus and allocative efficiency. Refer to both graphs.

_____
_____
_____
_____
_____
_____
_____
_____
_____
_____
_____
_____
_____
_____
_____
_____
_____
_____
_____
_____
_____
_____
_____
_____
_____
_____
_____
_____
_____
_____
_____
_____

Question four: Subsidy and elasticity

Complete **a** and **b** to explain the impact of a subsidy on allocative efficiency in the market when goods or services are either price elastic or price inelastic.

Diagram 1: Inelastic demand

Diagram 2: Elastic demand

a Complete the table below, use labels:

		Diagram 1	Diagram 2
(i)	The new price		
(ii)	The new quantity		
(iii)	The change in consumer surplus		
(iv)	The change in producer surplus		
(v)	The deadweight loss		
(vi)	The cost of the subsidy to the government		

b Compare and contrast the impact of a per unit sales tax on allocative efficiency when goods or services have different elasticities.

Explain the change in consumer surplus, producer surplus and allocative efficiency. Refer to both graphs.

_____

_____

_____

_____

_____

_____

_____

_____

_____

_____

_____

_____

_____

_____

_____

_____

_____

_____

_____

_____

_____

_____

_____

_____

_____

_____

_____

_____

_____

_____

Question five: Trade and different time periods

a Explain fully the change in consumer surplus and producer surplus in the **short run** when there is an increase in the world price. Use labels and refer to your diagram.

Diagram 1: Short run (inelastic) supply for a product

Diagram 2: Long run (elastic) supply for a product

_____

_____

_____

_____

_____

_____

_____

_____

_____

_____

_____

_____

_____

b Contrast and compare the impact on allocative efficiency in the **short run** with the **long run** that results from an increase in the world price to Pw2.

Explain the impact on allocative efficiency in both time frames and shade the change in allocative efficiency on both diagrams.

Explain why there is a greater change in allocative efficiency in the long run when compared to the short run.

Support your answer and refer to the labels on both diagrams.

_____

_____

_____

_____

_____

_____

_____

_____

_____

_____

_____

_____

_____

_____

_____

_____

_____

_____

_____

_____

_____

_____

_____

_____

_____

_____

_____

_____

_____

_____

_____

Question six: Subsidy

Subsidy and the market

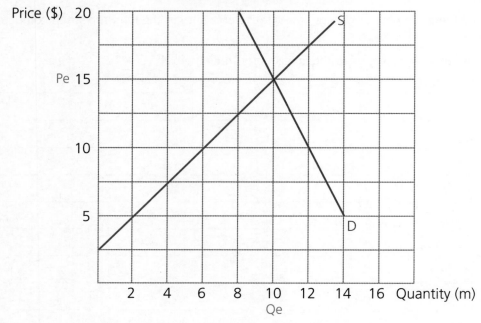

a (i) On the diagram illustrate the effect of a $7.50 per unit subsidy. Label the new equilibrium price as **Pc**, the new quantity as **Qc** and the price that producers now receive per item as **Pp**.

(ii) Explain how market forces move the market to the new equilibrium. Refer to the diagram in your answer.

_____

_____

_____

_____

_____

_____

_____

_____

_____

_____

_____

b Calculate the values of:

(i) Change in consumer surplus_____

(ii) Change in producer surplus _____

(iii) Cost of the subsidy to the government _____

(iv) Deadweight loss _____

c Explain the impact of a subsidy on consumer surplus, producer surplus and allocative efficiency. Refer to your calculations in **b**.

_____

_____

_____

_____

_____

_____

_____

_____

_____

_____

_____

_____

_____

_____

_____

_____

_____

_____

_____

_____

_____

_____

_____

_____

Question seven: Goverment decisions

Diagram 1
Market for cigarettes – a sales tax

Price ($) per packet

33
30 — S
27
24
21
18
15
12
9
6 — D

5   10   15   20   25   30   35   Quantity (millions)

a   On Diagram 1 illustrate the effect of a per unit tax that results in an equilibrium price of $21 per packet of cigarettes. Label the new equilibrium price as **Pc**, the new quantity as **Qc** and the price that producers now receive per item as **Pp**.

b   Complete the calculations of the government imposing an indirect tax (show your working) for **Diagram 1**:

   (i)   The change in consumer surplus _____

   (ii) The change in producer surplus _____

   (iii) The tax revenue for the government _____

c   The government decides to set a minimum price at $21 per packet of cigarettes. Complete the calculations (show your working) for **Diagram 2**:

   (i)   The change in consumer surplus _____

   (ii) The change in producer surplus _____

   _____

   (iii) The change in consumer spending _____

d Compare and contrast the impact of a minimum price with a policy of an indirect tax on the market for cigarettes, on consumer surplus, producer surplus and the government. Use the calculations you have made.

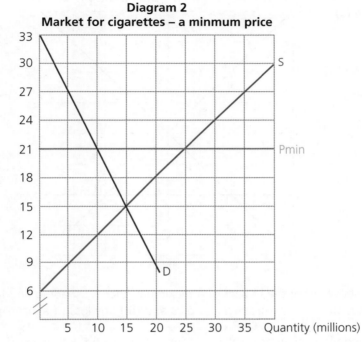

Diagram 2
Market for cigarettes – a minmum price

_____

_____

_____

_____

_____

_____

_____

_____

_____

_____

_____

_____

_____

_____

_____

_____

_____

_____

_____

_____

_____

_____

Question eight: Goverment policies

Market for milk – maximum price

a On Diagram 1 above show the impact of a maximum price by shading and labelling **(i)** the new consumer surplus **(ii)** the new producer surplus and **(iii)** any loss of allocative efficiency.

b Explain the change in consumer surplus, producer surplus and allocative efficiency.

_____

_____

_____

_____

_____

_____

_____

_____

_____

_____

_____

_____

_____

_____

_____

_____

_____

_____

_____

_____

       ISBN: 9780170438117

**Market for milk –
Goods and Service Tax removed**

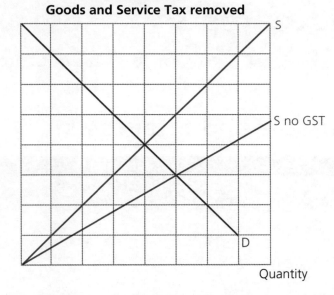

Price ($)

S

S no GST

D

Quantity

c   Compare and contrast the impact of a maximum price with a policy of removing GST on the milk market on consumer surplus, producer surplus and allocative efficiency. In your answer:

(i)   Label the original equilibrium price Pe and original equilibrium Qe. Label the new equilibrium price as Pn and new equilibrium quantity Qn on Diagram 2 above.

(ii) Shade and label the new consumer surplus and producer surplus.

(iii) Explain the change in CS, PS and allocative efficiency when the GST is removed.

(iv) Explain why removing GST would be more allocatively efficient that imposing a price control.

Refer to both diagrams.

_____

_____

_____

_____

_____

_____

_____

_____

_____

_____

_____

_____

_____

_____

_____

_____

_____

_____

_____

16 COSTS
Basic concepts

Fixed, variable and total costs

Costs for a firm			
Output or quantity (Q)	Fixed Costs ($) FC	Variable Costs ($) VC	Total Costs ($) TC = FC + VC
0	250	–	250
1	250	70	320
2	250	120	370
3	250	140	390
4	250	160	410

The table above shows the typical costs faced by a firm. **Fixed costs (FC)** are **independent of output**, they must be paid whether or not the firm is producing, e.g., rent, mortgage repayments, rates. These are costs that a firm cannot avoid and must pay because they involve contractual arrangements with other parties, even if the firm closes down. Fixed costs (FC) are a constant amount regardless of the level of output (that is, they will not change).

Fixed costs can possibly change in the long run, e.g., the council sets new rates, firms arrange new terms of interest and repayment on loans or mortgages, or rent arrangements come up for review.

Variable costs (VC) represent **costs directly related to production** and will change as output increases or decreases, for example, power, raw materials, postage, wages. If there is no production, variable costs will be zero.

Total cost (TC) refers to the total expense firms incur to produce a certain level of output. Total cost is made up of total fixed costs (TFC or FC) and total variable costs (TVC or VC). When a firm is not producing (zero output) total costs are made up entirely of fixed costs because fixed costs are independent of output. The firm does not have any variable costs at zero output because variable costs are dependent on production and therefore are only incurred when a firm is producing.

The drawing of the typical-shaped curves for variable cost, fixed cost and total costs is shown in the diagram below. The total cost (TC) curve is similar in shape to the variable cost (VC) curve, but starts at the fixed cost (FC) curve. The vertical distance between TC and VC at any level is equal to FC. The fixed cost (FC) curve is drawn as a horizontal line.

Costs for a firm

TC = FC plus VC.
The variable cost curve (VC) is parallel to the total cost curve and sits below the total cost curve by the amount equal to the value of fixed costs (FC).

       ISBN: 9780170438117

1 a Complete the table.

Quantity	FC ($)	VC ($)	TC ($)
1			720
2			1 000
3		830	1 230
4		1 000	1 400
5		1 100	1 500
6			1 900
7	400		

b Label the curves using the information from the table, use the small boxes for your answers.

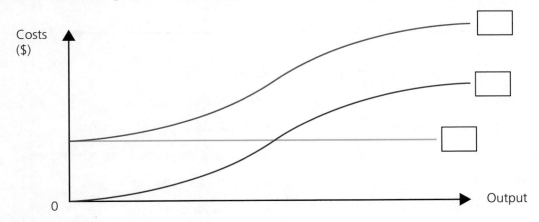

c What are a firm's variable costs (VC)?

_____

_____

_____

_____

d What are a firm's fixed costs (FC)?

_____

_____

_____

_____

_____

_____

_____

2 **a** Complete the table.

Quantity	FC ($)	VC ($)	TC ($)
0			400
1			1 040
2		750	1 150
3		800	

b Draw the typical shapes of the total cost, fixed cost and variable cost curves.

Costs ($)

0 → Output

c Write whether the following 'costs' are fixed or variable.

(i) Rates _____

(ii) Hire purchase repayments _____

(iii) Electricity _____

(iv) Workers' wages _____

(v) Raw materials _____

(vi) Stamps, postage requirements _____

(vii) Toll calls _____

(viii) Salaries _____

(ix) Interest repayments on a mortgage _____

(x) Insurance payments _____

(xi) Gas for cars _____

(xii) Rent for an office _____

d What is meant by the term total cost (TC)?

_____

_____

_____

_____

_____

_____

_____

_____

_____

_____

_____

_____

_____

    ISBN: 9780170438117

Costs for a firm			
Output Q	Fixed Costs FC ($)	Variable Costs VC ($)	Total Costs TC ($)
0		–	5 000
1			6 400
2			7 400
3		2 800	
4		3 200	
5		3 800	
6			9 600

3 a Complete the table.

b Give a formula that could be used to calculate total fixed costs.

_____

_____

_____

_____

_____

c Give a formula that could be used to calculate total variable costs.

_____

_____

_____

_____

d Give a formula that could be used to calculate total cost.

_____

_____

_____

_____

17 COSTS
Shapes of the curves

Cost curve shapes

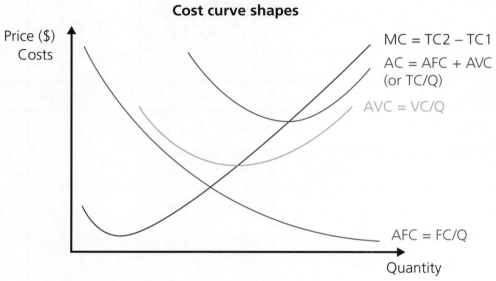

$$MC = TC2 - TC1$$
$$AC = AFC + AVC$$
(or TC/Q)
$$AVC = VC/Q$$
$$AFC = FC/Q$$

The average fixed cost (AFC) curve

Fixed costs (FC) are **independent of output**, they must be paid whether or not the firm is producing, e.g., rent, mortgage repayments, rates. These are costs that a firm cannot avoid and must pay because they involve contractual arrangements between other parties, even if the firm closes down. Fixed costs (FC) are a constant amount regardless of the level of output (that is, they will not change).

Output (Q)	Fixed costs ($)	Average fixed costs (AFC = FC/Q) ($)
0	800	–
1	800	800.00
2	800	400.00
3	800	266.67
4	800	200.00
5	800	160.00
6	800	133.33
7	800	114.29

Average fixed costs (AFC) equals fixed costs divided by quantity. Therefore, average fixed costs multiplied by quantity equals fixed cost. A change in a component of fixed costs will shift the fixed cost curves (total fixed costs and average fixed costs), total cost curve and average cost curve but leave the variable cost curve and the marginal cost curve unchanged.

As output increases, the average fixed cost curve (AFC) continuously falls from a maximum and tends towards zero because fixed costs are spread over a greater output.

         ISBN: 9780170438117

Marginal cost (MC)

Marginal cost (MC) is the addition to total costs of an extra unit of output.

The typical **shape of the MC curve** is shown in the graph. Initially increasing returns and the more efficient use of resources leads to falling marginal costs. However, in the short run eventually marginal costs increase because of diminishing returns. The law of **diminishing returns** refers to the idea that as more and more of a factor (input) is used, with at least one fixed factor, there is some point at which the increase in output will be at a decreasing rate. Each variable unit produces less when diminishing returns are occurring, so the production of extra units of output will require more and more of the variable inputs (compared to earlier units). Therefore, it follows that the cost of each additional unit produced (ie, MC) must increase because more inputs are being used to produce it.

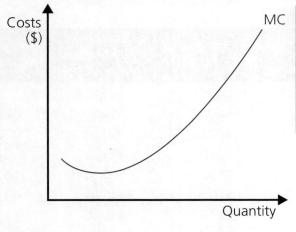

Output (Q)	Total cost (TC)	Marginal cost (MC)
0	660	–
1	920	260
2	1 100	180
3	1 320	220
4	1 760	440

To calculate marginal cost you work out the difference between total cost and the previous total cost. **Marginal cost will equal (Total Cost 2) minus (Total Cost 1)**. The marginal cost of the third unit in the table is $220 because it is the difference between the total cost of the third unit ($1320) and the total cost of the previous (second) unit produced ($1100).

If the total cost of 121 units is $12 093.95 and the total cost of production of 120 units is $12 000, the marginal cost is the difference between the total cost of 121 units and the total cost of the previous 120 units produced. In this instance the marginal cost will equal $12 093.95 minus $12 000 which is $93.95.

Given that total costs equals average costs multiplied by quantity, then marginal costs will equal (AC2 multiplied by Q2) minus (AC1 multiplied by Q1). For example, if the AC of 101 units is $19.95 and the average cost of 100 units is $20, the marginal cost equals (101 multiplied by $19.95) minus (100 multiplied by $20). Therefore, marginal costs equals $2 014.95 minus $2 000 which is $14.95.

Total costs equals fixed costs plus variable costs (TC = FC plus VC). Fixed costs are independent of output and do not change while variable costs are dependent on production, then the difference in total costs, which equals marginal cost, must be the difference between variable costs of the current output and the previous output. Given that marginal costs (MC) equals (FC plus VC2) minus (FC plus VC1), then MC must equal VC2 minus VC1. Marginal costs contain no fixed costs because fixed costs are a constant, the change in total costs must equal the change in variable costs.

Average total costs (ATC or AC) and average variable costs (AVC)

Variable costs (VC) represent **costs directly related to production** and will change as output increases or decreases, for example, power, raw materials, postage, wages. If there is no production, variable costs are zero.

A change in a component of variable costs will shift the variable cost curves (total variable costs and average variable costs), marginal costs and the total cost curve but leave the total fixed cost curve and the average fixed cost curve unchanged.

Variable costs divided by quantity equals average variable costs (AVC). Therefore, average variable costs multiplied by quantity equals variable costs.

Output (Q)	Fixed costs (FC)	Variable Costs (VC)	Total Costs (TC)	Average fixed costs (AFC = FC/Q)	Average variable costs (AVC = VC/Q)	Average costs (AC = TC/Q)
0	800	–	800	–	–	
1	800	640	1 440	800.00	640.00	1 440.00
2	800	1 200	2 000	400.00	600.00	1 000.00
3	800	1 660	2 460	266.67	553.33	820.00
4	800	2 000	2 800	200.00	500.00	700.00
5	800	2 200	3 000	160.00	440.00	600.00
6	800	3 000	3 800	133.33	500 00	633.33
7	800	4 800	5 600	114.29	685.71	800.00

Average total costs (ATC or AC) are the total costs divided by output.

Cost curves for a firm

The average cost curve (ATC) is equal to average fixed costs (AFC) plus average variable costs (AVC). **The shape of the ATC (AC)** is therefore **derived from the shapes of the AFC and AVC curves**, and is **typically U shaped**.

As output increases, the AFC continuously falls because fixed costs are spread over a greater output. Intially, the AVC falls due to efficient resource use but at some stage diminishing returns set in causing the AVC to increase (because additional inputs are required to produce the additional output). Since both AFC and AVC fall initially, this causes the ATC curve to slope downward. At some stage however, as output increases, the AVC increases faster than the AFC falls, causing the ATC curve to slope upward.

As output increases the gap between AC and AVC narrows (gets closer). Average fixed costs (AFC) declines with increasing output because fixed costs (FC) are spread over a greater number of units of output. Since AC equals AFC plus AVC, a higher proportion of total costs (TC) will be made up of variable costs (VC) as output rises, so the gap narrows.

The rising section of the marginal cost curve intersects both the average cost curve and the average variable cost at their minimum (lowest) points. The AC and AVC curves must be drawn cutting MC at their minimum (lowest) points.

Average and marginal cost curve

Costs ($)

If AC are less than MC (or MC > AC), then the AC are rising

MC

AC

When AC = MC, AC is at a minimum point. This is the technical optimum.

If AC are greater than MC (or MC < AC) then the AC are falling.

Output

When marginal costs are less than average costs, then average costs must be falling because the extra cost of producing the next unit is less than the average cost.

When marginal costs are greater than average costs, then average costs must be rising because the extra cost of producing the next unit is greater than the average, therefore where AC equals MC, AC is minimised (the technical optimum).

Cost curve relationships

Cost curve relationships		
Cost curve to calculate	**Formula**	**Rearranging the formula**
Average fixed costs (AFC)	AFC = FC/Q	AFC x Q = FC
Average variable costs (AVC)	AVC = VC/Q	AVC x Q = VC
Average costs (AC or ATC)	AC = TC/Q	AC x Q = TC
Marginal costs (MC)	MC = TC2 – TC1	MC + TC1 = TC2 TC1 = TC2 – MC

QUESTIONS & TASKS

1 Complete each table and label the curves indicated by the title of each graph.

Output units	FC ($)	AFC ($)
0	100	–
1	100	
2	100	
3	100	
4	100	
5	100	

Output units	FC ($)	VC ($)	TC ($)
0	100	0	100
1		100	
2		160	
3		200	
4			325
5			335
6			390
7			520

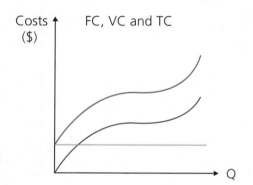

Output units	VC ($)	TC ($)	AVC ($)	AC ($)
0	0	100	–	–
1	100	200	100	200
2	160	260		
3	200	300		
4	225	325		
5	235	335		
6	290	390		
7	420	520		

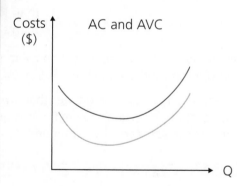

Output units	TC ($)	AC ($)	MC ($)
0	100	0	–
1	200	200	100
2	260	130	60
3	300		
4	325		
5	335		
6	390		
7	520		

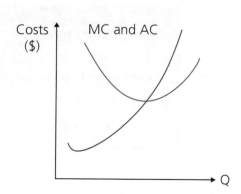

2 **a** Draw an accurate AFC cost curve and explain why AFC continually decline as output increases.

_____

_____

_____

_____

b Write correct or incorrect next to the following statements.

(i) TC = AC x Q _____ **(viii)** TC = AFC + AVC _____

(ii) TC = FC + VC _____ **(ix)** AFC = FC x Q _____

(iii) AFC = FC ÷ Q _____ **(x)** AC = TC ÷ Q _____

(iv) AC = AFC + AVC _____ **(xi)** AVC = VC x Q _____

(v) AVC = VC ÷ Q _____ **(xii)** FC + VC = AC _____

(vi) AFC + AVC = AC _____ **(xiii)** TC ÷ Q = AC _____

(vii) AC x Q = TC _____ **(xiv)** (AFC + AVC) x Q = TC _____

c If you were informed that the average cost was $9 and 100 units were produced, what is the total cost?

_____

d Complete the table.

Quantity	Fixed costs ($)	Variable costs ($)	Total costs ($)	Average total costs ($) = $\frac{TC}{Q}$
400	200		3 400	
		4 000		8.4

e At 1 200 units AVC equals $10.16 and AFC are $0.83. Use this information to work out total costs, fixed costs and variable costs.

_____

_____

_____

_____

3 a Label all the curves in the graph.

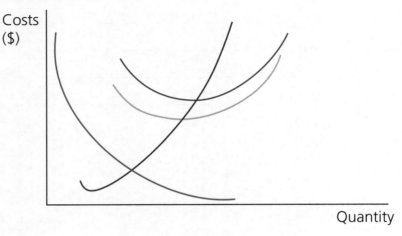

b Distinguish between marginal and average costs.

_____

_____

c (i) What cost concept is represented by the vertical gap between AC and AVC? _____

(ii) Explain why this gap narrows as output rises.

_____

_____

_____

_____

d Why does the MC curve intersect the AC curve at its minimum point?

_____

_____

_____

e Complete each table.

(i)

Quantity	AC ($)	TC ($)	MC ($)
100	20.00		
101	19.95		

(ii)

Quantity	TC ($)	MC ($)	AC ($)
6	48	13	
7		15	

4 **a** Explain the shape of the marginal cost curve.

_____

_____

_____

_____

_____

b Work out the marginal cost if the average cost of 2 000 units is $200 and of 2 001 units $199.95.

_____

_____

c Use the table to answer the questions that follow.

(i) Complete the table.

Output (Q)	Total costs (TC) ($)	Average costs (AC) ($)	Marginal cost (MC) ($)
0	660	–	–
1	920	920	
2	1 100		
3	1 320		
4	1 760	440	
5		484	
6		660	

(ii) What is the technical optimum output of this firm, and how did you establish this position?

_____

(iii) Complete these formulae.

TC ÷ Q = _____   AC x Q =   _____

FC + VC = _____   (AFC + AVC) x Q = _____

(iv) At zero output what is the value of FC and VC for this firm? Give reasons for your answer.

_____

_____

_____

_____

d Define 'marginal cost'.

_____

_____

_____

Typical costs for a firm					
Output (Q)	Fixed costs (FC) ($)	Variable costs (VC) ($)	Total costs (TC) ($)	Marginal costs (MC) ($)	Average costs (AC) ($)
0	100	–	100	–	–
1					200
2					130
3					100
4	100				81
5					67

5 Compare and contrast the typical cost curves for a firm. In your answer you should:

- Complete the missing values in the table above and draw a sketch to show the following cost curves: MC, AC, AVC and AFC.
- Distinguish between marginal and average costs.
- Explain why the gap between the AC and AVC cost curves narrows as output increases.
- Explain why the MC curve intersects the AC at its minimum point.

_____

_____

_____

_____

_____

_____

_____

_____

_____

_____

_____

_____

_____

_____

_____

_____

_____

_____

_____

_____

_____

_____

_____

PHOTOCOPYING OF THIS PAGE IS RESTRICTED UNDER LAW.   ISBN: 9780170438117

6 A taxi driver is on duty at the airport one night. The usual taxi fare for the 50 kilometre trip from the airport to the city is $25.00. A potential passenger offers the taxi driver $15.00 for the trip. The driver has fixed costs of $500 per week and variable costs of 30 cents per kilometre.

Explain to the taxi driver about the typical costs for a firm. In your answer you should:

- Complete the missing values in the table below.
- Define fixed costs and variable costs and state a likely example of each for a taxi driver.
- Draw a sketch diagram to show a firm's MC, AC and AVC curves.
- Explain why the gap between the AC and AVC narrows as output rises.

Q	FC ($)	VC ($)	TC ($)	AC ($)	AFC ($)	AVC ($)	MC ($)
0	500	–	500	–	–	–	–
1			640	640	500	140	140
2			740	370	250	120	
3		280		260	166.67	93.33	
4		320					40
5		380	880			76	60
6		460	960	160	83.33	76.67	80

_____

_____

_____

_____

_____

_____

_____

_____

_____

_____

_____

_____

_____

_____

_____

_____

_____

_____

_____

_____

_____

Cost curves for a firm

7 a Use the graph above to complete the statement. Justify your answer.

The total cost for a firm at 200 units is _____ and the total fixed costs are _____.

_____

_____

_____

_____

b Complete the table.

Situation		Impact on average costs	Direction marginal cost curve will shift (inward, outward or not at all)
(i)	An increase in fixed costs.		
(ii)	An increase in salaries.		
(iii)	A decrease in rent paid when a new premises is found.		
(iv)	A decrease in variable costs.		
(v)	A decrease in wages.		
(vi)	An increase in variable costs.		
(vii)	An increase in the price of raw materials.		

c Complete the statement. Justify your answer.

An increase in costs that are directly related to output for a firm will increase a firm's _____

_____ and _____.

_____

_____

_____

_____

_____

_____

_____

8 a Complete the statement. Justify your answer.

When the marginal cost is below average cost, average costs are _____. When the marginal cost curve is above average cost, average costs are _____. Where average costs equal marginal costs, average costs are _____.

_____

_____

_____

_____

b (i) Label the curves below.

(ii) Draw a new average cost curve (AC2) to show the effect on a firm of an increase in fixed costs.

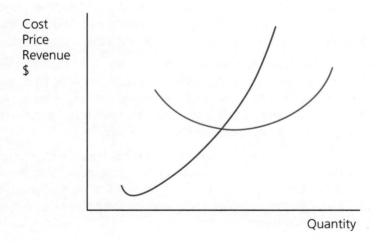

c (i) Label the curves below.

(ii) Draw a new average cost curve (AC2) and marginal cost curve (MC2) to show the effect on a firm of a decrease in variable costs.

Features of perfect competition

Perfect competition is a market situation in which no firm or individual is able to influence the working of the market. Firms are small in size and exist in large numbers. Perfect competitors are **price takers**, because they are too small to influence price.

Firms produce **identical (homogeneous) products** and there are **no barriers to entry**, with anyone who wishes, able to set up in business.

The market structure also requires **perfect knowledge** meaning that firms know about prices of inputs and technology available and buyers have knowledge of price of finished goods and services, for example market gardens, orchardists, dairy farmers, maize growing. Christmas tree sellers might be considered perfect competitors if one tree is considered to be the same as the next.

An individual firm in perfect competition can sell as much as it desires at the ruling market price. Total revenue will increase steadily with sales, while the additions to total revenue (the marginal revenue) that results from each additional sale will be constant. Therefore, marginal revenue will equal price because all units are sold for the same price (MR = P). Average revenue is the same as price and doesn't change with output sales, since all units are sold at the same price.

The individual perfect competitor faces a horizontal demand curve because their supply is relatively small compared to the quantity supplied by the entire industry; they are able to sell all that they supply at the ruling market price. The industry demand curve is downward sloping because it represents the sum of all individual consumer demand curves at each price for the good of an industry and shows that additional quantities will be purchased at lower prices.

Revenue curves for perfect competition

Revenue for a perfect competitor can be divided into total revenue, average revenue and marginal revenue.

Total revenue (TR) is the revenue received from all sales. Total revenue equals price multiplied by the quantity (P × Q). A key relationship with revenue curves is that price equals average revenue (P = AR) because price and average revenue are calculated from total revenue.

Average revenue (AR) is the total revenue received from sales divided by the number of units sold. Average revenue equals total revenue divided by quantity (TR ÷ Q).

Marginal revenue (MR) is the change of total revenue resulting from increasing sales by one unit, that is, it's the addition to the total revenue of the firm as the result of the sale of an additional unit of output. Marginal revenue equals TR2 minus TR1.

An individual firm in perfect competition can sell as much as it is desires at the ruling market price. Total revenue will increase steadily with sales, while the additions to total revenue (the marginal revenue) that result from each additional sale will be constant. Marginal revenue will equal price because all units are sold for the same price (MR = P).

Average revenue is the same as price and doesn't change with output sales, since all units are sold at the same price (AR = P).

     ISBN: 9780170438117

Revenue for a firm in perfect competition is illustrated in the schedule and graph below.

Quantity Q	Price (P) $	Total revenue (TR) ($)	Average revenue (AR) ($)	Marginal revenue (MR) ($)
Revenue for a perfect competitor				
1	50	50	50	50
2	50	100	50	50
3	50	150	50	50
4	50	200	50	50
5	50	250	50	50

TR = P x Q

AR = TR/Q   P = TR/Q   AR = P

MR = TR2 – TR1

AR = P = MR = D

The diagrams show that the individual firm in Graph two accepts the market price set in Graph one. The individual perfect competitor faces a horizontal demand curve because their supply is relatively small compared to the quantity supplied by the entire industry; they are able to sell all that they supply at the ruling market price. The industry demand curve is downward sloping because it represents the sum of all individual consumer demand curves at each price for the good of this industry.

Marginal cost pricing is a feature of perfect competition. It is a situation in which price is equal to marginal cost (P=MC). Sellers cannot charge higher prices, i.e., mark-up price over cost, because they would immediately lose sales to competitors. This is called marginal cost pricing and occurs only in perfect competition.

1 a Complete the table for a perfect competitor and then draw the curve indicated by the title of each graph.

Output	Price ($)	TR ($)	AR ($)	MR ($)
1	20		20	
2	20	40		
3	20			
4				20
5		100		

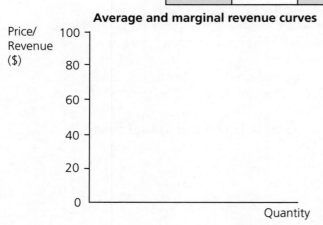

Average and marginal revenue curves

Price/Revenue ($)

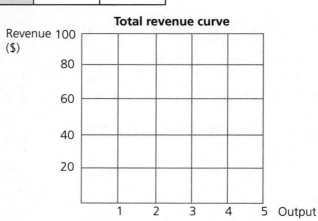

Total revenue curve

Revenue ($)

b Indicate which statements below are correct for perfect competition. (Use the table and graph in question **1a** to assist you.)

(i) All units are sold at $20. _____   **(ii)** MR > Price   _____

(iii) Price = AR   _____   **(iv)** AR = demand   _____

(v) Price > MR   _____   **(vi)** TR increases then falls. _____

c Explain why a perfect competitor's AR and MR curves are drawn as a horizontal line.

_____

_____

_____

d What are the features of an individual firm in perfect competition?

_____

_____

_____

Dairy farmers have been enjoying excellent returns in recent years.
Forestry, sheep and beef farm units have recently been converted into
dairy units in the expectation that high returns will continue.

2 a What is the relationship between a perfectly competitive dairy farm and the market supply of dairy products?

_____

_____

b List three characteristics of a perfectly competitive firm that could apply to a dairy farm.

_____

_____

_____

c Is the demand curve faced by an individual firm in perfect competition the same as the market demand curve? Why or why not?

_____

_____

_____

_____

_____

_____

_____

_____

_____

_____

d Use the diagram to explain how Graph 1 and Graph 2 illustrate perfectly competitive competition.

Graph 1: The individual firm

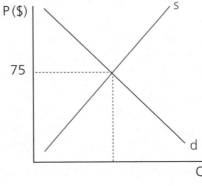

Graph 2: The market (industry)

_____

_____

_____

_____

_____

19 PROFIT

Economic and accounting costs

Accounting costs are the actual (or explicit) costs involved in the production process – mortgage, rent, power, office expenses, raw materials and wages. Accounting costs represent the costs of production that a firm will pay to other businesses. Accounting costs will always be less than economic costs.

Economic costs are the actual (explicit) or accounting costs as well as the opportunity costs (implied or implicit) of the resources used.

Implicit or implied costs are the opportunity costs of the resources used that are owned by the business. Economic costs represent the revenue that could be earned in alternative uses of assets that the firm owns, this would include the amount foregone by the owners that they could have earned working for a different business, for example, the lost salary of a teacher who starts a cafe. This would include the rent lost by the owner(s) of a factory whose firm currently uses the building, or the lost interest that could have been earned by the owner(s) if they had the funds in a bank account rather than being lent to the business.

Some producers will have higher economic costs than other producers because they own a larger proportion of the resources used in the production process when compared with other firms.

Economists use economic costs rather than accounting costs when determining the profit maximising level of output for a firm, because to calculate their profit maximising level of output, firms must know their total costs. Economic costs provide a total cost that includes all the costs of production including opportunity costs. Accounting costs do not cover opportunity costs, such as the return on the risk taken by the entrepreneur, and therefore do not cover all costs. Economic costs are always greater than accounting costs.

Economic and accounting profit

Explicit costs involve a monetary payment made by a firm to its suppliers, workers or others involved in running a business. Implicit costs, on the other hand, do not involve any payment being made to others.

Accounting profit is calculated as profit equals income minus expenses, where the expenses or costs are only the actual (or explicit) costs involved. So, in accounting terms, a 'profit' or surplus exists if the actual income of the business is greater than the actual expenses. Accounting profit is always greater than economic profit.

In economics, both actual costs and implied (or opportunity) costs are included in the calculation of profit. Therefore, economic profit equals the accounting profit minus the implicit or implied (opportunity) costs incurred by the business. There will always be opportunity costs involved in any business venture, so the economic profit for a business will always be less than the accounting profit.

For example, a teacher leaves his job and opens a cafe using his $100,000 from a savings account, that was earning 7% per annum. The teaching job had paid $60,000. The income from the cafe was $120,000 and costs were $40,000 after the first year. Therefore, the accounting profit is $80,000 because the accounting profit is the income of $120,000 minus the costs of $40,000.

The business has incurred two opportunity costs in operating the cafe, namely the lost salary of $60,000 by the owner and the interest lost of $7,000 (based on 7% of $100,000) that could have been earned on the savings had the savings not being used to start the cafe. The economic profit equals the accounting profit minus the opportunity costs. In this instance, the economic profit is $13,000 because economic profit equals the accounting profit of $80,000 minus the opportunity costs of $67,000. The economic profit of $13,000 is less than the accounting profit of $40,000.

    ISBN: 9780170438117

Total revenue and total cost

The difference between total revenue (TR) and total cost (TC) is either a profit or loss. A firm that wants to maximise its profit or minimise its loss would operate at the output shown in the graphs.

Maximising profit

If a firm wants to maximise profit it would operate where there is the greatest vertical distance between TR and TC. This is shown on the graph as position Q. Any other position would result in a smaller profit, and if the firm operated beyond Q' it would make a loss.

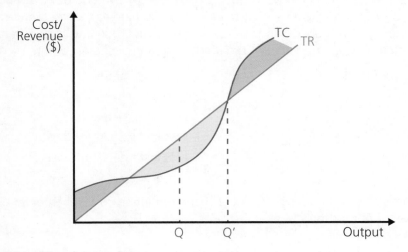

Minimising a loss

In the graph there is no position in which the firm can make a profit at this stage of its operation. To minimise its loss it would operate where the vertical distance between the total revenue (TR) and the total cost (TC) is the smallest. This is at output Q. Any other position would result in a greater loss.

QUESTIONS & TASKS

1 a Complete the table below.

Hagar Backpackers Accommodation was started by Hagar with $40 000 of his savings. Hagar had given up his job of teaching where he used to earn $35 000 per year. Market interest was 5% on deposits. After the first year's operation total revenue was $300 000 and total expenses $240 000. Use this information provided to work out the accounting and economic profit.

Accounting profit	$		Economic profit	$
Income	_____		Income	_____
Expenses	_____		Less actual expenses	_____
Net profit	$_____		Less lost wages	_____
			Less lost interest on savings	_____
			Net profit	$_____

b Why do economists use economic costs rather than accounting costs when determining the profit maximising level of output for a firm?

_____

_____

_____

_____

_____

_____

_____

c Economic costs cover more than accounting costs. Give two specific examples of non-accounting costs likely to be incurred by an owner of a backpackers.

_____

_____

_____

d Define the following terms.

(i) Accounting profit: _____

_____

(ii) Economic profit: _____

_____

_____

ISBN: 9780170438117

2 a (i) Complete the table and answer the questions that follow.

Quantity (000)	Total revenue ($000)	Total cost ($000)	Profit/Loss ($000)
0	–	145	loss 145
1	180	175	profit 5
2	320	200	profit 120
3	420	220	
4	480	250	
5	500	300	
6	480	370	
7	420	460	loss 40

(ii) According to the table, at what output would you recommend that this firm operate and why?

_____

b (i) Complete the table and answer the questions that follow.

Output (000)	TR ($000)	TC ($000)	Profit/Loss ($000)
5	25	40	
6	30		12 loss
7	35	45	
8		46	6 loss

(ii) According to the information in the table, what type of market structure is the firm? Give a reason for your answer.

_____

(iii) From the information in the table, what would you recommend that this firm do and why?

_____

_____

Adrian's previous job as a real estate agent paid $60 000. Adrian uses $40 000 from a term deposit earning 5% per annum to start up a concrete pumping business.
Accounting costs for the year $150 000   Total revenue $250 000

c Study the information given above then calculate the accounting profit and economic profit for Adrian who started off a business pouring concrete.

(i) Accounting profit: _____

(ii) Economic profit: _____

_____

d Which is greater, accounting profit or economic profit?

_____

e Which is greater – accounting costs or economic costs?

_____

3 A business faces accounting costs and economic costs.

a Explain the difference between accounting costs and economic costs.

_____

_____

_____

_____

_____

_____

_____

_____

_____

_____

_____

b Label the following costs explicit or implicit.

(i) Actual costs of production _____

(ii) Economic costs _____

(iii) Implied costs _____

(iv) Accounting costs _____

(v) Opportunity costs of interest foregone _____

(vi) Wages for factory workers _____

(vii) Rent lost for the building owned and used by the producer _____

(viii) Interest on the bank overdraft _____

(ix) Salary of the general manager _____

4 a Complete the table below assuming it represents a perfectly competitive firm and the current market price is $10.

Output (Q)	Average cost (AC) ($)	Total cost (TC) ($)	Total revenue (TR) ($)	Profit (or loss) ($)
8 000	2.10			
10 000	2.50			
12 000	5.00			

b Why do economists use economic costs rather than accounting costs when determining the profit maximising level of output for a firm?

_____

_____

_____

_____

_____

_____

_____

c Indicate whether the following statements are correct or incorrect.

Statement		Correct or incorrect?
(i)	Economic profit is always greater than accounting profit.	
(ii)	Accounting profit is always greater than economic profit.	
(iii)	Economic profit is always smaller than accounting profit.	
(iv)	The correct measure of economic cost includes explicit and implicit cost.	
(v)	The correct measure of economic cost includes accounting costs and opportunity costs.	
(vi)	Accounting profit is a firm's revenue minus explicit costs only.	
(vii)	Economic profit is a firm's revenue minus explicit costs only.	
(viii)	Actual costs are implicit costs of the opportunity costs in operating a business.	
(ix)	Implicit costs are the actual costs of a firm.	
(x)	Explicit costs are the actual costs of a firm.	
(xi)	Total revenue equals sales (or quantity) times price.	

Marginal analysis – Perfect competition

The **rule for maximising profit or minimising a loss (the equlibrium)** is where **marginal revenue (MR) equals marginal cost (MC)**. Any other position will result in a smaller profit or greater loss.

Therefore, the equilibrium output (determined from the intersection of the marginal cost and marginal revenue curves) is at a price of $200 and quantity Q (200). The **average revenue (AR)** equals $200 and the **average cost (AC)** equals $160.

Total revenue (TR) equals the quantity multiplied by the price or average revenue (**Q × AR**). In this case it equals 200 multiplied by $200 which equals $40 000.

Total cost (TC) will equal the quantity multiplied by the average cost (**Q × AC**). In this case it equals 200 multiplied by $160 which equals $32 000.

At the **equilibrium output Q** the firm is making a **supernormal profit** of $8 000. **Supernormal profit** is a return more than sufficient to keep the entrepreneur in their present activity. At the equilibrium output position where MR equals MC, the average revenue (AR) is greater than the average cost (AC). Supernormal profits will attract firms into a perfectly competitive industry because there are no barriers to entry.

If output is **below equilibrium Q** (MR equals MC), the firm would be **missing out on marginal profits** because the revenue from producing the last article is greater than its cost of production, implying that the firm could increase output and increase profit.

However, increasing output **beyond Q** reverses the position. The firm will be **making marginal losses** because the revenue from one additional article is now less than the cost of its production. If increased output adds more to cost than to revenue, a firm has obviously passed the point of maximum profit (or minimum loss). Therefore the rule is adopted and applies in all circumstances where profit maximisation is the aim.

Subnormal profit

Subnormal profit is a return insufficient to keep the entrepreneur in their present activity. At the equilibrium output position where MR equals MC, average revenue (AR) will be less than average cost (AC). When a firm is making a subnormal profit it is likely that they will leave the industry.

Q (200) is the equilibrium output position because this is where MR equals MC. At an output of 200, the price (AR) is $200, the average cost (AC) is $260, the total revenue is $40 000 (AR multiplied by Q) and the total cost is $52 000 (AC multiplied by Q).

Subnormal profit for a perfect competitor

Normal profit

Normal profit in economic terms is a return to the entrepreneur sufficient to keep them in their present activity. At the equilibrium output position where MR equals MC, the average revenue (AR) will equal the average cost (AC).

Q (200) is the equilibrium output position because this is where MR equals MC. At an output of 200, the price (AR) is $200, the average cost (AC) is $200, the total revenue is $40 000 (AR multiplied by Q) and the total cost is $40 000 (AC multiplied by Q).

Normal profit for a perfect competitor

1 Work out the answers to the questions by using the graphs provided.

Perfect competition

Revenue/Costs ($)

TC
TR

25 000

12 500

0   5 000   Quantity

a The maximum profit position is at an output of _____ because this is where the gap between the total revenue curve and the total cost curve is the _____ distance.

Marginal approach

Revenue/Costs ($)

8.00 — MC

AC

5.00 — MR = AR = P = D
4.00
2.50
2.10

0   4   5   6   Quantity (000)

b (i) Shade and label the appropriate level of profit made at the equilibrium level of output (maximum profit).

(ii) Complete the table.

Value	4 000 units	5 000 units	6 000 units
(i) MR/MC			
(ii) AR/AC			
(iii) TR (AR x Q)			
(iv) TC (AC x Q)			
(v) PROFIT			

c Using the idea of marginal analysis, explain why the firm would not want to operate at either 4 000 or 6 000 units.

_____

_____

_____

_____

_____

_____

2 Use the graph to answer the questions that follow.

An individual firm's costs curves and revenue curve

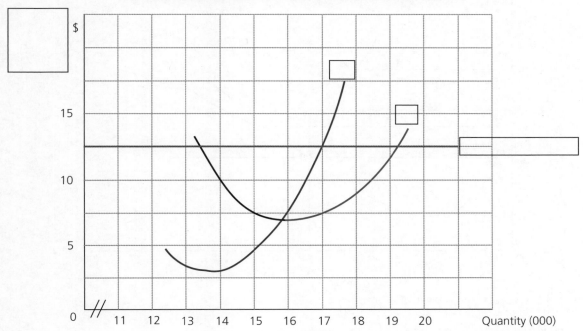

a Label all the curves and the vertical axes in the graph, using the small boxes for answers.

b Using a marginal analysis, what is the maximum profit position price and output?

Price: _____ Output: _____

c At the equilibrium output position calculate total revenue and total cost.

Total revenue (AR x Q): _____

Total cost (AC x Q): _____

d Shade in the area of profit.

e Work out the value of profit.

_____

f **(i)** If the firm was operating at 15 000 units, what price would they charge?

_____

(ii) Give values for MR and MC _____

(iii) What would the firm have to do to maximise profit in terms of price and output?

_____

_____

_____

_____

_____

_____

_____

3 Use the graph to answer the questions below.

a Label the curves and axes in the graph.

b Give letters and values to identify at the equilibrium:

(i) Output _____

(ii) Price _____

(iii) TC _____

(iv) Quantity _____

(v) TR _____

(vi) Loss _____

(vii) AC _____

(viii) AR _____

c What made you choose the equilibrium output above?

_____

_____

d In the graph, shade in the economic profit made.

e Define this type of profit.

_____

_____

_____

_____

 ISBN: 9780170438117

4 Use the diagram to answer the questions that follow.

a Label all the curves and shade in the profit made.

b At the maximum profit (equilibrium output) position, what is the:

Price? _____ Total revenue? _____

Output? _____ Total cost? _____

Average revenue? _____

c By considering outputs 9 000, and 10 000 units, explain using marginal analysis the determination of the maximum profit output level.

_____

_____

_____

d What type of profit is made in the diagram? _____

e Define this type of profit.

_____

_____

_____

_____

f Explain why the firm would not want to operate at 12 000 units.

_____

_____

_____

_____

_____

_____

_____

5 Use the diagram to answer the questions that follow.

a Label the curves.

b (i) Identify the loss-minimising level of output as Q and price charged as P.

_____

(ii) What made you choose this position?

_____

c Shade in the loss made.

d At 50 000 units:

identify average revenue   _____

identify marginal revenue   _____

calculate total revenue   _____

calculate total cost   _____

calculate loss made   _____

e At 40 000 units:

identify average revenue   _____

identify marginal revenue   _____

calculate total revenue   _____

calculate total cost   _____

calculate loss made   _____

6 Use the graph to answer the questions that follow.

a Define 'subnormal profits'.

_____

_____

_____

_____

b Label the curves on the diagram above.

c (i) Identify loss minimising level of output as QM.

_____

(ii) At the loss minimising level of output what is AR? _____

TR? _____

TC? _____

loss? _____

d Shade in the loss made.

e (i) Why would the firm not produce at 50 000 units?

_____

(ii) At 50 000 units what is AR? _____

TR? _____

TC? _____

loss? _____

21 REVENUE CURVES
Monopoly

Imperfect competition

Firms are subdivided into monopolistic, oligopoly, duopoly, monopoly, and monopsony. Imperfect competitors produce differentiated products and have a varying degree of control over price. They are price makers because of their ability to make their products appear different, that is, relative to their competitors their products are not homogeneous. For any imperfect competitor to sell an additional unit they must lower the price. Therefore, as output increases, to sell an additional unit the price will fall. A decrease in output will see price increase.

Monopoly (or monopolist)

Single seller of good or service for which there are few if any substitutes, for example Kiwi Rail the only railway in New Zealand and New Zealand Steel the only steel producer in the country. Monopolies have strong barriers to entry in the same way that oligopolies do. Pure monopoly implies that there are no substitutes while a near monopoly is one with relatively few substitutes. For example Kiwi Rail has a pure monopoly in rail transport but it is only a near monopoly in transport. Limitations on monopolistic power include:

- due to consumers' incomes being limited, all commodities are in competition with each other so they cannot be too exorbitant in their pricing;

- government can break up monopolies or control their prices if they become too high; they could nationalise them and run them in the public's best interest.

A monopolist can set either price or quantity but not both in the market. If the monopolist sets the price the market will determine the quantity sold. If the monopolist determines the quantity then the market will determine the price. The monopolist has control over price or quantity produced, but not over both at the same time.

Barriers to entry — Monopoly power

Most firms face competition from existing firms that produce the good or provide the service. When barriers to entry to a market are either weak or non-existent new firms can enter the market, establish themselves and claim market share for the goods or service. This is not the case for a monopoly because they are the single seller of a good or service for which there are few, if any, substitutes, this situation arises because the strong barriers to entry restrict the entry of would-be competitors.

The strong barriers to entry for a monopoly range from **high establishment costs, technological expertise, legal monopolies** established by the government or barriers that arise from economies of scale in the instance of a natural monopoly.

Competitors are often kept out of an industry where a monopolist operates because of the enormous expense of setting up in the first place. In the case where a rail monopoly exists a would-be competitor would face the high capital cost of buying the land required for a rail corridor, laying down of tracks, building stations, buying trains and rolling stock, as well as any other associated expenses. The high capital cost involved in setting up would be a major deterrent to most firms.

Another barrier that protects a monopoly from competition is the technological expertise that a monopolist possesses. If a monopolist has developed technology by spending vast sums on Research and Development that only they have knowledge of and access to, this can make it difficult, if not impossible, for competitors trying to produce the same goods or provide the same service because they lack either the necessary skills needed or knowledge to do so. The time and expense for other firms to develop the expertise required helps maintain the monopolist's position in keeping competitors out of a market. Patents and copyright can protect a firm from competitors for a time, however, these measures may not be effective in the long term because new technology is developed or a competitor finds a way to circumvent a registered patent.

       ISBN: 9780170438117

Revenue curves

Revenue for an imperfect competitor can be divided into total revenue, average revenue and marginal revenue.

Total revenue (TR) is the revenue received from all sales. Total revenue equals price multiplied by the quantity (P × Q). A key relationship with revenue curves is that price equals average revenue (P=AR) because price and average revenue are calculated from total revenue.

Average revenue (AR) is the total revenue received from sales divided by the number of units sold. Average revenue equals total revenue divided by the quantity (TR ÷ Q). Average revenue (AR) falls in line with price changes, i.e., AR equals Price.

Marginal revenue (MR) is the change of total revenue resulting from increasing sales by one unit, that is, it's the addition to the total revenue of the firm as the result of the sale of an additional unit of output. Marginal revenue equals TR2 minus TR1. Marginal revenue should be plotted midway between consecutive units of output.

In any form of imperfect competition, to sell additional units requires that the price be lowered on all units. Therefore, for a decrease in price to sell an additional unit, the marginal revenue must be less than the price for which the prevoius unit is sold. The marginal revenue curve must lie beneath the average revenue curve for imperfect competition. It follows that average revenue (AR) or price (P) is always greater than marginal revenue (MR) in imperfect competition. A firm's demand curve in imperfect competition is its average revenue (AR) curve.

With the fall in price total revenue (TR) will reach a maximum and then fall thereafter. When total revenue (TR) reaches a maximum, marginal revenue (MR) equals zero (0). After this point, as output increases and the price decreases marginal revenue will become negative.

Revenue for a firm in imperfect competition is illustrated in the schedule and graph below. Note the marginal revenue curve cuts the output axis exactly halfway between the origin and where the average revenue curve cuts the output axis.

Revenue for an imperfect competitor				
Quantity Q	Price (P) $	Total Revenue (TR) ($)	Average Revenue (AR) ($)	Marginal Revenue (MR) ($)
1	250	250	250	250
2	200	400	200	150
3	150	450	150	50
4	100	400	100	−50
5	50	250	50	−150

TR = P x Q

AR = TR/Q P = TR/Q AR = P

MR = TR2 − TR1

AR > MR

Revenue curves for imperfect competition

In **imperfect competition** the seller is able to charge a price in excess of marginal cost. This is called **mark-up pricing** and is where price is greater than marginal cost (P > MC).

QUESTIONS & TASKS

1 Complete the table by selecting your answer from the following: monopoly, AR (P), TR, imperfect competition, AR = MR, AR > MR or (MR < AR), MR, perfect competition, AR curve.

	Idea, formula, definition	Answer
a	To sell an additional unit the firm must lower its price	
b	Price stays the same for the individual firm because it is too small to influence price	
c	P x Q	
d	TR ÷ Q	
e	Demand curve of the perfect or imperfect competitor equals its …	
f	Many sellers of an identical product implies …	
g	An industry consisting of only one firm	
h	The relationship for perfect competitors' AR and MR curves	
i	The relationship for imperfect competitors' AR and MR curves	
j	Any change in quantity results in no change in the price received by a firm	
k	Additions to the total revenue of a firm as a result of sale of an additional unit of output	
l	Price multiplied by quantity	
m	Total revenue divided by quantity	

2 Label the curves fully and give each diagram a title.

PHOTOCOPYING OF THIS PAGE IS RESTRICTED UNDER LAW.   ISBN: 9780170438117

3 a Complete the table and use the information to answer part **b**.

Quantity	Price ($)	TR ($)	MR ($)	AR = P ($)
1	36	36	36	36
2	32	64	28	32
3	28	84	20	28
4	24	96	12	24
5	20	100	4	20
6	16	96	−4	16
7	12	84	−12	12

b Label the curves and complete each statement.

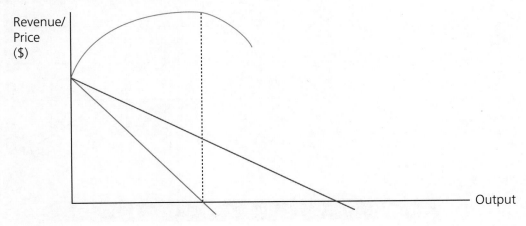

Revenue/Price ($)

Output

(i) When TR is a maximum, MR is _____.

(ii) When TR is falling, MR is a _____ number.

c What are the features of a perfect competitor?

_____

_____

_____

_____

d What are the features of a monopolist?

_____

_____

_____

_____

_____

_____

_____

_____

_____

4 Use the diagram to answer the questions that follow.

a Draw an accurate MR curve.

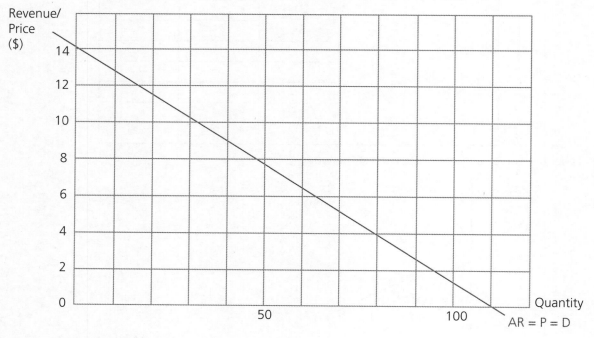

AR = P = D

b Complete the table.

Output	Price ($)	Total revenue ($)	AR ($)
20	11.50		
50			7.80
80	3.90		
95		190	

c Complete these statements.

(i) In imperfect competition, as a firm increases its output price will _____, e.g., an increase output from 20 to 95, price will _____ from _____.

(ii) In imperfect competition, as a firm decreases output then price will _____, e.g., in decreasing output from 80 to 50 will see price _____ from _____.

d Complete the following statements.

(i) An increase in output for an imperfect competitor will see price _____.

(ii) A decrease in output for an imperfect competitor will see price _____.

(iii) The change in output and price for an imperfect competitor occurs in _____ directions.

(iv) Price will rise in imperfect competition when output _____.

(v) Price will fall in imperfect competition when output _____.

(vi) Price will not _____ for firms in _____ even if there is an increase or decrease in output.

 ISBN: 9780170438117

5 Use the graph below to answer the questions that follow.

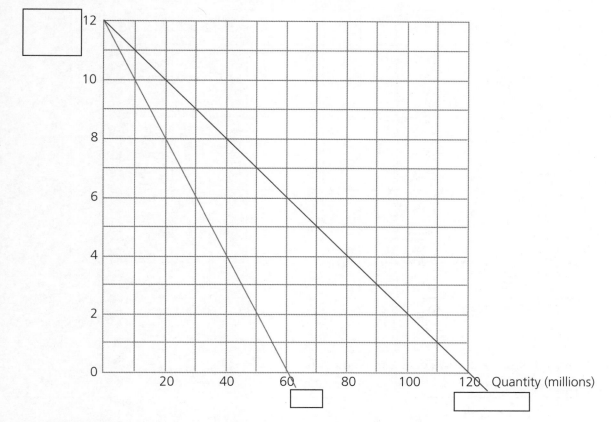

a Label all the curves and axes appropriately, using the small boxes for answers.

b Explain how the revenue curves illustrate imperfect competition.

_____

_____

_____

c Define marginal revenue.

_____

_____

d (i) Complete the table using the information above.

Units	Price (AR) ($)	Total revenue (TR) ($)	Marginal revenue (MR) ($)
20 million			
40 million			
60 million			
80 million			−4

(ii) Indicate at which level of output total revenue is a maximum and describe the relationship between TR and MR at this point.

Output: _____

Relationship: _____

6 **a** Label the curves and the axes and then answer the questions that follow.

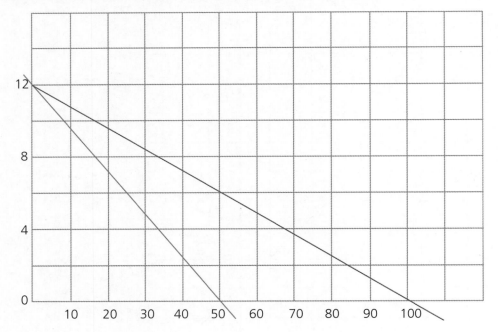

b What kind of demand curve does a monopolist face?

_____

_____

c At a price of $11, how many units can a monopolist sell? What is their total revenue?

Units sold = _____   TR = _____

d If the price is lowered to $6, how many units can the monopolist sell? What is their total revenue?

Units sold = _____   TR = _____

e Indicate if the following statements are correct or incorrect for the imperfect competitor.

Statement	Correct or incorrect?
(i) When a firm in imperfect competition increases output, price will increase.	
(ii) When a firm in imperfect competition increases output, price will decrease.	
(iii) When an imperfect competitor produces less, then price will decrease.	
(iv) When an imperfect competitor produces less, then price will increase.	

f Explain why a monopolist is able to set either market price or market quantity, but not both.

_____

_____

_____

_____

_____

_____

       ISBN: 9780170438117

7 Perfect competitors and imperfect competitors have different revenue curves.

Compare and contrast revenue curves for various market structures. In your answer:

- Label the curves and explain how the revenue curves illustrate imperfect competition.
- Explain why a monopolist is able to set either market price or market quantity, but not both.
- Explain why the average revenue curve is horizontal for a perfect competitor but slopes downward for a monopolist.

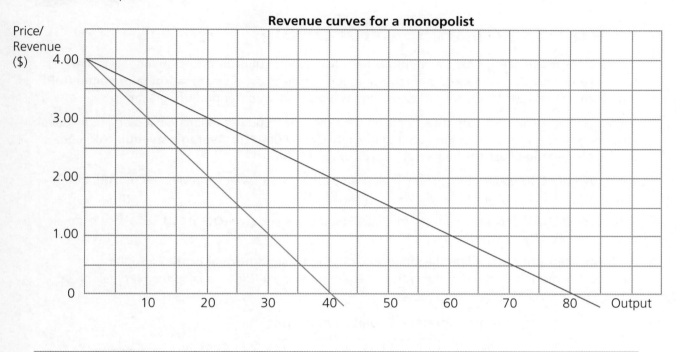

Revenue curves for a monopolist

_____

_____

_____

_____

_____

_____

_____

_____

_____

_____

_____

_____

_____

_____

_____

_____

_____

_____

_____

Marginal analysis – Monopoly

The **rule for maximising profit or minimising a loss (the equlibrium)** for a monopoly is the same as any other firm. The most profitable output or smallest loss is where **marginal revenue (MR) equals marginal cost (MC)**. Any other position will result in a smaller profit or greater loss.

Therefore, the equilibrium output (determined from the intersection of the marginal cost and marginal revenue curves) is at a price of **Pm** ($8) and quantity **Qm** (200m). The **average revenue (AR)** equals $8 and the **average cost (AC)** equals $5.

Total revenue (TR) equals the quantity multiplied by the price or average revenue **(Q × AR)**. In this case it equals 200m multiplied by $8 which equals $1600m.

Total cost (TC) will equal the quantity multiplied by the average cost **(Q × AC)**. In this case it equals 200m multiplied by $5 which equals $1000m.

At the **equilibrium output Qm** the monopoly is making a **supernormal profit** of $600m. Supernormal profit is a return to the entrepreneur more than sufficient to keep them in their present activity.

In imperfect competition, for a firm to sell an additional unit it must lower price. If the firm operates **below the equilibrium output**, it is **missing out on marginal profits** because its marginal revenue is greater than its marginal costs (or marginal costs are less than marginal revenue). Therefore, to maximise profits (or to minimise loss) the firm will need to increase output to where MR equals MC, as output increases price will fall.

If an imperfect competitor firm operates **beyond the equilibrium output**, it is **making marginal losses** because its marginal cost is greater than its marginal revenue (or marginal revenue is less than marginal cost). Therefore, to maximise profits (or to minimise loss) the firm will need to decrease output back to where MR equals MC, as output decreases the price will increase.

Subnormal profit

Subnormal profit is a return insufficient to keep the entrepreneur in their present activity. At the equilibrium output position where MR equals MC, average revenue (AR) will be less than average cost (AC).

Q (5m) is the equilibrium output position because this is where MR equals MC. At an output of 5m, the price (AR) is $9, the average cost (AC) is $11, the total revenue is $45m (AR multiplied by Q) and the total cost is $55m (AC multiplied by Q).

Subnormal profit for an imperfect competitor

Normal profit

Normal profit in economic terms is a return to the entrepreneur sufficient to keep them in their present activity. At the equilibrium output position where MR equals MC, the average revenue (AR) will equal the average cost (AC).

Q (5m) is the equilibrium output position because this is where MR equals MC. At an output of 5m, the price (AR) is $9, the average cost (AC) is $9, the total revenue is $45m (AR multiplied by Q) and the total cost is $45m (AC multiplied by Q).

Normal profit for an imperfect competitor

QUESTIONS & TASKS

1 Use the graphs to complete the tables.

Total revenue and total cost approach to profit

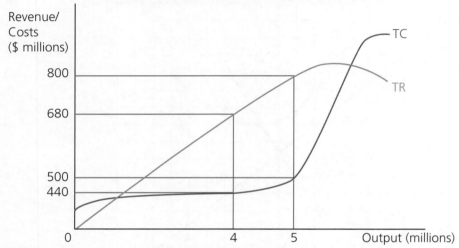

a

Output (millions)	Total revenue (TR) ($m)	Total costs (TC) ($m)	Profit ($m)
4			
5			

Marginal approach to profit

b

Value	Output of 4 million	Output of 5 million
MR		
MC		
AR		
AC		
TR (AR x Q)		
TC (AC x Q)		
Profit		

c Shade in and label the area of profit at the equilibrium output.

       ISBN: 9780170438117

2 Use the diagram to answer the questions that follow.

Costs and revenue curves for imperfect competition

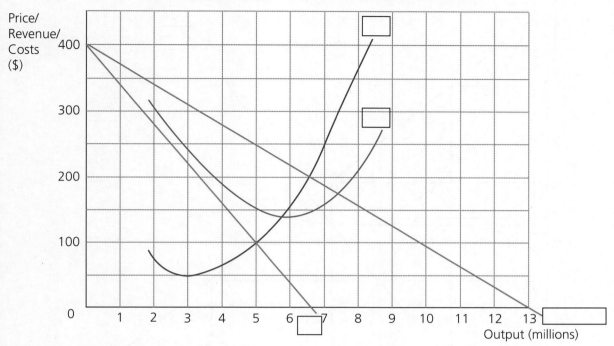

Price/Revenue/Costs ($)

Output (millions)

a Label the curves on the graph, using the small boxes for answers.

b According to the marginal analysis, at what output and price is profit maximised?

Output: _____   Price: _____

c At the equilibrium output position calculate total revenue and total cost.

Total revenue (AR x Q): _____

Total cost (AC x Q): _____

d Shade in the area of profit.

e Work out the value of profit.

_____

f (i) If the firm was operating at 3 million units, what price would they charge?

_____

(ii) Give approximate values of MR and MC:

_____

_____

(iii) What must the firm do to maximise profits in terms of both price and output?

_____

_____

_____

_____

_____

_____

3 Use the diagram to answer the questions below.

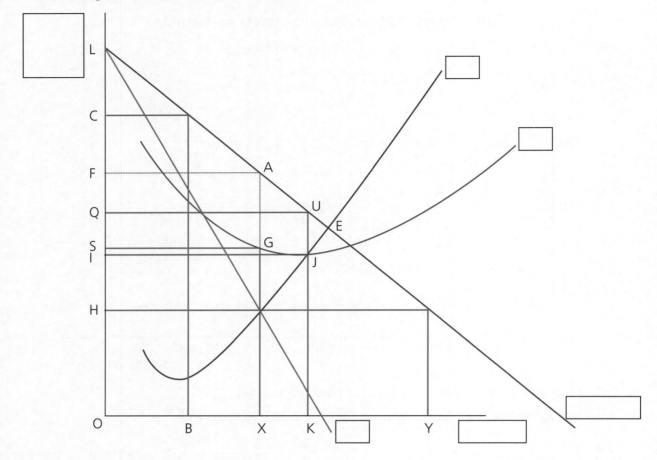

a Label the curves and axes, use the small boxes provided. Label the equilibrium price and quantity as PM and QM respectively. Shade and label the area of profit made.

b Give letters to represent the following at the maximum profit position.

Price: _____   Total revenue _____

Output: _____   Total cost _____

Average cost _____   Profit _____

c Explain, using the terms 'marginal losses' and 'marginal profits', why the firm would not choose to operate at OB or OY.

_____

_____

_____

_____

_____

_____

_____

_____

_____

_____

_____

4 a Draw an imperfect competitor making supernormal profits in the diagram shown. Label the axes fully and then identify the equilibrium output as Q and price charged as P. Shade in the area of profit.

b Use the diagram below to answer the questions that follow.

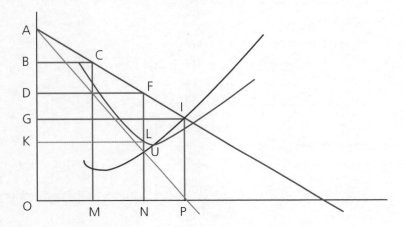

(i) Label the curves and axes.

(ii) Shade in the profit made.

(iii) Give letters to identify the following at the profit maximising position.

Output _____   TR _____

Price _____   TC _____

AR _____   Profit _____

(iv) In terms of profit maximising what is happening at OP?

_____

_____

_____

_____

_____

_____

_____

_____

5 Equilibrium output is where MR = MC.

Explain why equilibrium output is where MR = MC. In your answer you should:

- Label all the curves on the diagram below and calculate the monthly supernormal profit being made at the equilibrium output. Show your working.
- Show and label the area of supernormal profit made.
- Explain why the profit maximising price would be at the output you have indicated.

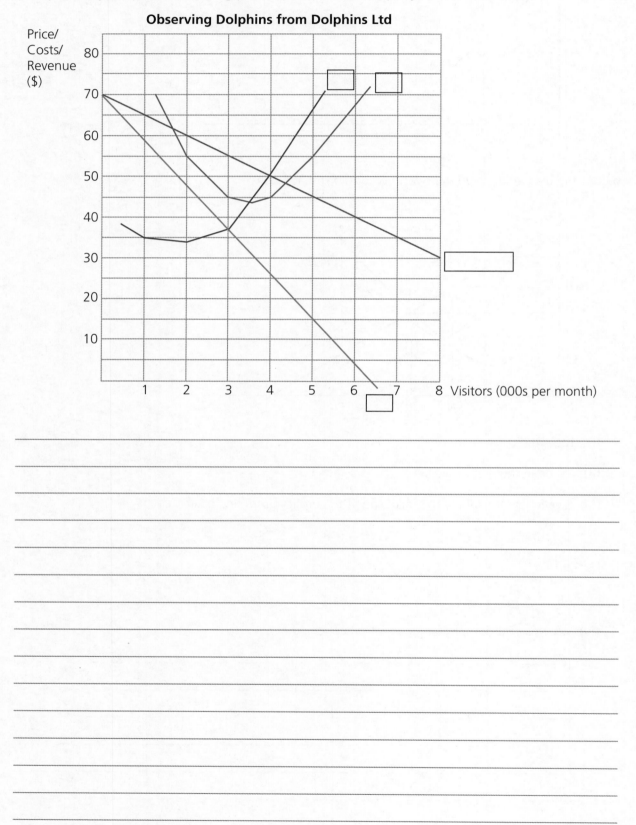

Observing Dolphins from Dolphins Ltd

_____

_____

_____

_____

_____

_____

_____

_____

_____

_____

_____

_____

_____

_____

_____

_____

6 The relationship between price and marginal revenue will determine a firm's market structure. Two firms have the following cost and revenue structures at an output level of 4 000 units.

Firm	Price	Marginal Revenue	Average Cost	Marginal Cost
X	$1.50	$1.20	$1.80	$2.00
Y	$0.75	$0.75	At its minimum level of $0.75	?

Explain how both firms can maximise profits. In your answer you should:

- Explain the profit maximising rule.
- Explain how we know Firm X is an imperfect competitor.
- Explain why Firm Y, a perfect competitor, should continue producing 4 000 units.

_____

_____

_____

_____

_____

_____

_____

_____

_____

_____

_____

_____

_____

_____

_____

_____

_____

_____

_____

_____

_____

_____

_____

_____

_____

_____

Pricing in perfect and imperfect competition

At the equilibrium output in **perfect competition** price and marginal cost are the same. Sellers cannot charge higher prices because they would immediately lose sales to competitors. This is called marginal cost pricing and occurs in perfect competition where price equals marginal cost (P = MC), and output is determined at the profit maximising position where MR = MC. This is shown in the diagram opposite.

In **imperfect competition** the seller is able to charge a price in excess of marginal cost. This is called **mark-up pricing** and is where price is greater than marginal cost (P > MC), and the output is also at the profit maximising position where MR = MC. This situation is shown in the diagram opposite.

The outcome that is favoured by consumers is assumed to be that under perfect competition because this outcome is allocatively efficient and as such best represents the desires of society. A monopoly is deemed to restrict output and charge a higher price than would perfect competition; this is seen in the diagram opposite, where PmQm represents the monopoly situation and PpQp the perfect competition situation. A perfect competitor would have a lower price and greater quantity.

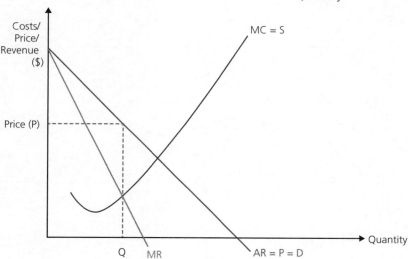

For society, insufficient resources are allocated to supply the quantity of goods or services that consumers demand; this is termed a loss of allocative efficiency or deadweight loss. This is shown as the shaded area in the diagram. This deadweight loss is a loss of welfare to individuals or society which is not offset by a welfare gain to some other individual or group.

A monopolist – various price regulations

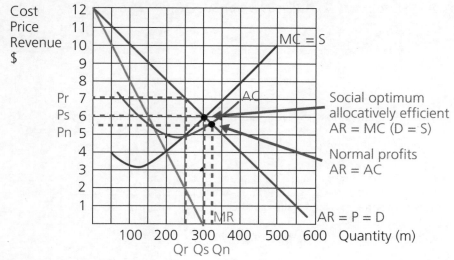

The government can regulate a monopoly by the administering of a price control that will not allow a monopolist to operate at the equilibrium. If a monopolist is regulated to a price of $7 (**Pr**) at an output of 250m (**Qr**) this is beyond the equilibrium position because marginal cost is greater than marginal revenue, the firm is making marginal losses on the increased output. The firm now makes a supernormal profit of $500m, this is less than the profit maximum position (or its most desired position). There is an increase in consumer surplus due to the lower price paid and higher quantity consumed by individuals. However, at Pr Qr the market is still not allocatively efficient because consumer surplus and producer surplus are not maximised but the deadweight loss is reduced.

A monopolist could be required or forced to **charge a price equal to marginal cost (P = MC)**. **Marginal cost pricing** results in the firm operating at the **social optimum** or **allocatively efficient** output position, in this case it is at a price of $6 (**Ps**) and an output of 300m (**Qs**). In a monopoly the average revenue curve is the market demand curve and the marginal cost curve is the supply curve for the good or service. At the new equilibrium position, the **deadweight loss is zero** (or eliminated) because the firm is operating where D (AR) = S (MC), the market is allocatively efficient because **consumer surplus and producer surplus are maximised**. At **Ps Qs** the monopolist is regulated to produce what a perfect competitor would produce and charge.

Average cost pricing regulates the firm to **charge a price equal to average costs (P = AC)**. In this instance the price would be $5.50 (**Pn**) and the quantity would be 325m units (**Qn**). The monopolist would not be maximising profits because the marginal revenue is less than marginal cost, the firm is making marginal losses on the increased output. The firm would make a **normal profit** instead of a supernormal profit. Normal profit is a return to the entrepreneur sufficient to keep them in their present activity.

Average cost pricing and marginal cost pricing both benefit consumers because they pay a lower price and receive a greater quantity than they would if the monopolist was allowed to operate at its preferred equilibrium output position.

Government ownership is an option, where a monopolist is owned and run by the government. The government can ensure that the monopolist acts in the public's best interest. In the private sector, inefficiency results in firms making a loss and leaving an industry. It is argued that state owned firms can be inefficient because there can be little incentive to be efficient and make profits. However, these enterprises today often operate along business lines and must return a dividend to the government, so they run as efficiently as any privatised firm.

1 a Complete the following statements, using marginal analysis (i.e., the relationship between MR and MC).

(i) Firms maximise profit where _____

(ii) Firms minimise loss where _____

(iii) Firms make a greater loss or smaller profit if they do not produce at where _____

(iv) A firm will decrease or increase output to where _____

b Complete the table.

Situation	Type of firm } Perfect Imperfect	Relationship between MC and MR
(i) To maximise its profit the firm must decrease its output and raise prices		
(ii) To maximise its profit the firm must decrease its output and price remains the same		
(iii)	Imperfect	MR < MC
(iv) To maximise its profit the firm has to lower its price and increase its output		
(v) To maximise its profit the firm has to leave output unchanged		
(vi) To maximise its profit the firm has to keep its price the same but increase its output		

c Complete the table for imperfect competition that desires to achieve equilibrium output.

Change in price	Change in output	Relationship between MC and MR
(i)		MC = MR
(ii)		MC > MR
(iii)		MR > MC

d Complete the table for a perfectly competitive firm that desires to achieve equilibrium output.

Change in price	Change in output	Relationship between MC and MR
(i)	increase	
(ii)	decrease	
(iii) do nothing	do nothing	

2 a Label the curves and shade in the profit made.

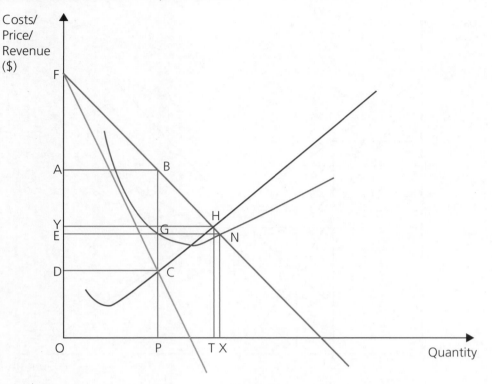

b Why are monopolies able to retain such supernormal profits?

_____
_____
_____
_____
_____
_____

c Give letters to identify the following at the profit maximum level.

(i) Consumer surplus (CS) _____   **(ii)** Average cost (AC) _____

(iii) Total revenue (TR) _____   **(iv)** Total cost (TC) _____

(v) Price _____   **(vi)** Deadweight Loss (DWL) _____

(vii) Profit _____

d Give letters to identify the price and output at the normal profit position.

Price _____   Output _____

e Give letters to identify the price and output at the social optimum position.

Price _____   Output _____

3 Use the diagram to answer the questions that follow.

a Label the curves and shade in the profit where MR = MC.

b If the government was to regulate this monopoly into making normal profits, what price would they charge and what is the output?

Price _____   Output _____

c At what price and output could the firm be regulated if price equals marginal cost?

Price _____   Output _____

d At which price and output would this firm be regulated to produce the same level of output and price if it wanted to achieve the social optimum level of production?

Price _____   Output _____

e Label the areas of consumer surplus (CS) and deadweight loss (DWL) and shade these in.

f Define deadweight loss.

_____

_____

_____

_____

_____

_____

4 Use the diagram to answer the questions that follow.

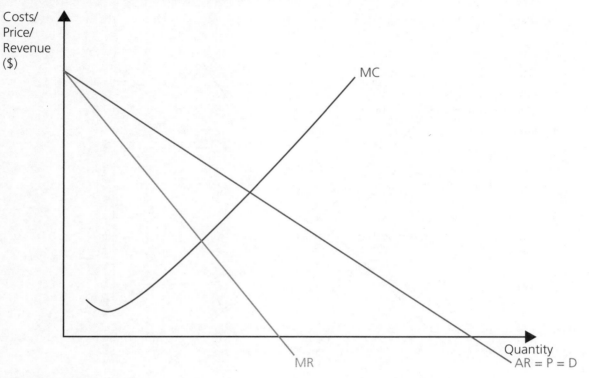

Costs/Price/Revenue ($) — MC — Quantity — AR = P = D — MR

a On the graph above:

(i) Label the profit maximising price (Pm) and quantity (Qm).

(ii) Draw an appropriately positioned average cost curve (AC) showing the monopoly firm earning normal profit.

b Justify the position of the average cost curve.

_____

_____

_____

c Explain why a monopolist is able to set either market price or market quantity, but not both.

_____

_____

_____

_____

_____

_____

d Explain why the average revenue curve is horizontal for a perfect competitor but slopes downward for a monopolist.

_____

_____

_____

_____

5 Use the graph to answer the questions below.

a (i) On the graph appropriately label all the curves and then identify the equilibrium level of output as **Qm** and identify the equilibrium price as **Pm**. Draw in an accurate MR curve and shade and label the profit made. Shade the deadweight loss.

(ii) Label the perfect competition price (**Pp**) and quantity (**Qp**).

b Explain, with reference to the diagram, why the outcome that is favoured by customers is **Qp**.

_____

_____

_____

_____

_____

_____

_____

_____

_____

_____

_____

_____

_____

_____

_____

_____

_____

_____

6 A monopoly is able to earn and retain supernormal profits in the long run.

Explain how a monoply is able to retain supernormal profits. In your answer you should:

- Label the curves on the diagram below and shade the supernormal profit made. Label the equilibrium output and price as **Qmax** and **Pmax**.
- Explain why long-run profits for a monopoly are likely to be different from those of a producer operating in perfect competition.
- Identify equilibrium price and quantity that would occur if the market was perfectly competitive.

Monopoly diagram

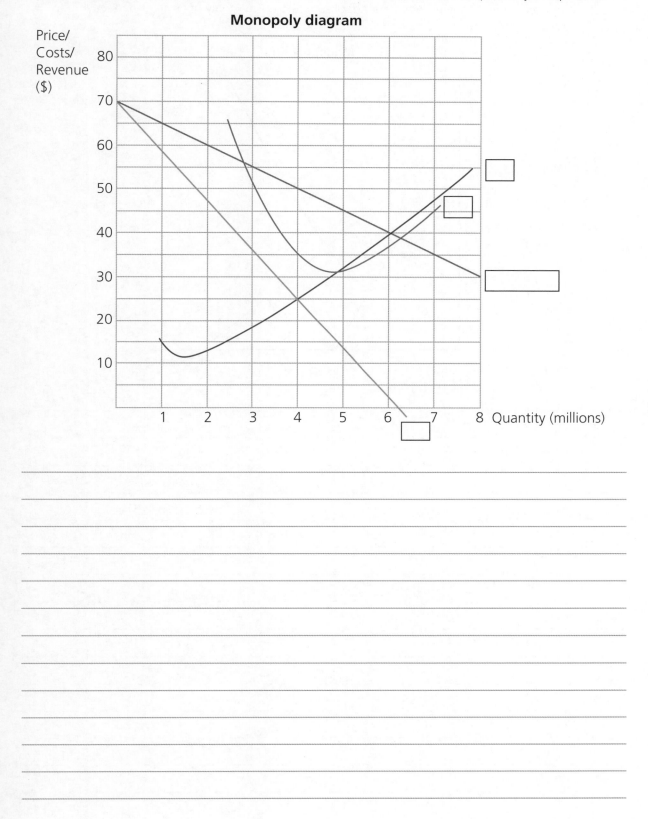

_____

_____

_____

_____

_____

_____

_____

_____

_____

_____

_____

_____

_____

7 A firm will aim to produce where MR = MC.

Fully explain a firm's output decision using marginal analysis. In your answer you should:

- Label the profit maximising price (**Pe**) and quantity (**Qe**) on the graph and add an appropriately positioned average cost curve (AC) showing the monopoly firm earning normal profit.
- Justify your positioning of your average cost curve.
- Identify the market price (Pps) and market quantity (Qps) that would occur if the graph showed a perfectly competitive market.
- Explain using marginal analysis why a monopolist would not willingly operate at perfectly competitive market output.

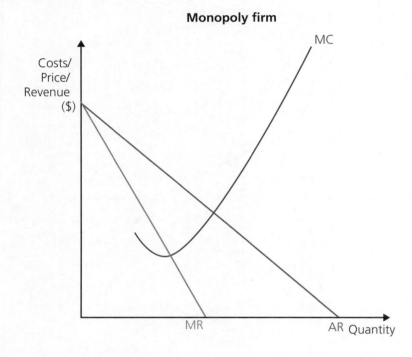

Monopoly firm

_____

_____

_____

_____

_____

_____

_____

_____

_____

_____

_____

_____

_____

_____

_____

_____

8 A monopolist will operate at the equilibrium output position.

Explain the equilibrium output position for a monopoly. In your answer you should:

- On Graph 1: draw a correctly positioned average revenue curve and label it AR = P = D; identify the monopoly firm's price (label it PM) and output (label it QM) and shade in the area showing the supernormal profit being earned.
- Show the effect that an increase in market demand has on the firm in the long run by carefully labelling any curve shifts, if necessary, to show the effect of an increase in market demand on a monopoly firm.
- Explain, using marginal analysis, the long-run output (i.e., QLR) shown on your diagram.

Graph 1: Monopoly firm

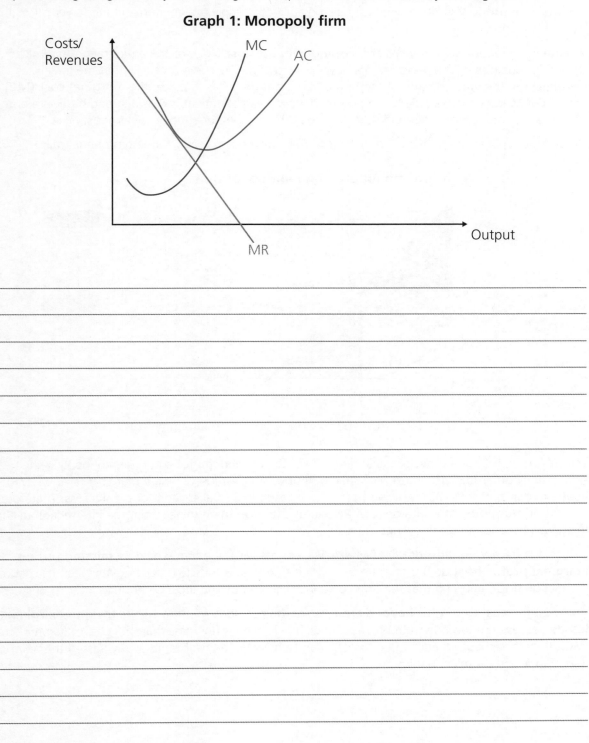

_____

_____

_____

_____

_____

_____

_____

_____

_____

_____

_____

_____

_____

_____

_____

_____

_____

_____

_____

_____

24 NATURAL MONOPOLY

Features of a natural monopoly

A **natural monopoly** is when one firm has the ability to supply the entire market at lower prices than two or more firms.

A natural monopoly faces **downward-sloping average cost (AC)** for the entire range for which demand is applicable. The reason for its downward-sloping AC curve is usually that the initial investment in the infrastructure of the firm is large, but once it is in place, the **marginal cost (MC)** of production is **low**, for example hydro power. This high establishment cost is a strong barrier to entry and a natural monopoly could undercut any would-be competitor so they could not survive.

Natural monopolies often involve some kind of **network**, for example water, gas,phone, rail.

A natural monopoly – equilibrium output

The rule for maximising profit or minimising a loss (the equlibrium) for a natural monopoly is the same as any other firm. The most profitable output or smallest loss is where marginal revenue (MR) equals marginal cost (MC). Any other position will result in a smaller profit or greater loss. Therefore, the **equilibrium output** is at a price of **Pe** and quantity **Qe** (determined from the intersection of the marginal cost and marginal revenue curves).

If output is **below equilibrium Qe (where MR equals MC),** the firm would be **missing out on marginal profits** because the revenue from producing the last article (MR) is greater than its cost of production (MC), implying that the firm could increase output and increase profit.

However, **increasing output beyond Qe** reverses the position. The firm will be **making marginal losses** because the revenue from one additional article (MR) is now less than the cost of its production (MC). If increased output adds more to cost than to revenue, a firm has obviously passed the point of maximum profit (or minimum loss).

Policies concerning natural monopoly

One way a government can regulate a monopoly is by administering **price controls** that do not allow a natural monopoly to operate at its preferred equilibrium output position where marginal revenue equals marginal cost. For this monopoly the equilibrium output is at a price of $7 (Pe) and quantity of 50m (Qe). The aim of price controls is to benefit the consumer with lower price and a greater quantity.

A natural monopoly – average cost pricing

Average cost pricing is a way that the government can improve resource allocation because it increases total surpluses in the market and reduces the deadweight loss that would be associated with a natural monopoly operating at its equilibrium position (MR = MC).

Average cost pricing regulates the firm to **charge a price equal to average costs (P = AC)**. In this instance the price would be $4 (**Pn**) and the quantity would be 80m units (**Qn**). The natural monopoly would no longer be maximising profits because the marginal revenue is less than marginal cost, the firm is making marginal losses on the increased output. The firm would make a **normal profit** instead of a supernormal profit. Normal profit is a return to the entrepreneur sufficient to keep them in their present activity. A natural monopoly regulated to a situation where price equals average cost is able to earn a fair rate of return.

The net **deadweight loss** to society is **reduced** but not eliminated, the deadweight loss is **now the area HKG**. The natural monopoly is making a normal profit so they may lack the funds to do R & D and be less innovative, this could be viewed as a negative impact on resource allocation of fixing the price. A price set to equal average cost is more socially desirable than the equilibrium output position because consumers experience a significant increase in consumer surplus due to the lower price and higher quantity consumed. Average cost pricing has the advantage over marginal cost pricing of not having to provide a subsidy to a natural monopoly to keep the firm operating.

A natural monopoly – marginal cost pricing

A natural monopoly could be required or forced to charge a price equal to marginal cost (P = MC). **Marginal cost pricing** results in the firm operating at the **social optimum** or **allocatively efficient** output position, in this case it is at a price of $2 (**Ps**) and an output of 100m (**Qs**). In a monopoly the average revenue curve is the market demand curve and the marginal cost curve is the supply curve for the good or service. At the new equilibrium position, the **deadweight loss is zero** (or eliminated) because the firm is operating where D (AR) = S (MC), the market is allocatively efficient because consumer surplus and producer surplus are maximised. At **Ps Qs** the natural monopoly is regulated to produce what a perfect competitor would produce and charge. However, the natural monopoly is making a **subnormal profit** shown by the shaded area. A subnormal profit is a return insufficient to keep the entrepreneur in their present activity, the firm would require a **subsidy** to continue operating in the long run.

Average cost pricing and marginal cost pricing both lower the price consumers pay and increase the quantity purchased. A natural monopoly operating at the equilibrium position creates a deadweight loss, average cost pricing reduces this deadweight loss while marginal cost pricing eliminates it. With marginal cost pricing a natural monopoly makes a subnormal profit and requires a subsidy to stay in business in the long run. Average cost pricing results in a natural monopoly making a normal profit that will mean it can stay in business in the long run without the need for a subsidy.

Government ownership is an option, where a natural monopoly is owned and run by the government. The government can ensure that the natural monopoly acts in the public's best interest. In the private sector, inefficiency results in firms making a loss and leaving an industry. It is argued that state owned firms can be inefficient because there can be little incentive to be efficient and make profits. However, these enterprises today often operate along business lines and must return a dividend to the government, so they run as efficiently as any privatised firm.

    ISBN: 9780170438117

1 Use the graph to answer the questions below.

a Label the curves and axes, using the small boxes for answers. Shade in and label the area of profit made and DWL.

b Give letters to identify at the profit maximising level of output.

Price _____   Total cost _____

Output _____   Profit _____

Average cost _____   Total revenue _____

c What is the distinguishing feature of a natural monopoly?

_____

_____

_____

_____

_____

d Tick (✓) which of the following are likely to be natural monopolies.

(i) New Zealand Steel ☐   **(iv)** Water distribution network ☐

(ii) Rail ☐   **(v)** Power generation ☐

(iii) Telecommunications ☐

2 Use the graph to answer the questions below.

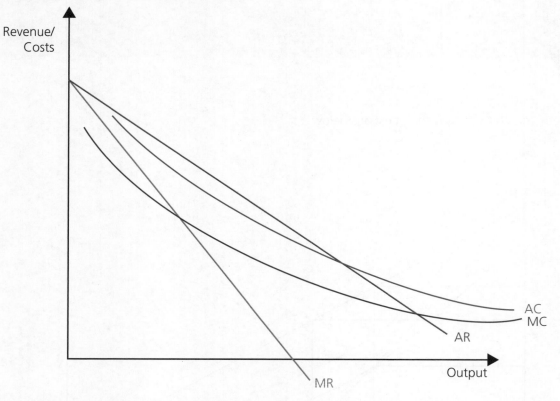

a **(i)** The government wishes to regulate the monopoly so that the socially optimum level of production is achieved. Identify the correct price and level of output. Label them P2 and Q2.

(ii) Shade and label the profit made at P2 and Q2.

(iii) What problem would be created in the long term? How could it be solved?

Problem _____

_____

Solution _____

_____

b Outline another method (apart from price controls) that the government could use to regulate the monopolist.

_____

_____

_____

c Give a reason why natural monopolies may be socially desirable, despite the fact that superprofits often exist.

_____

_____

_____

d Explain how economies of scale can lead to a natural monopoly.

_____

_____

     ISBN: 9780170438117

3 Use the graph to answer the questions below.

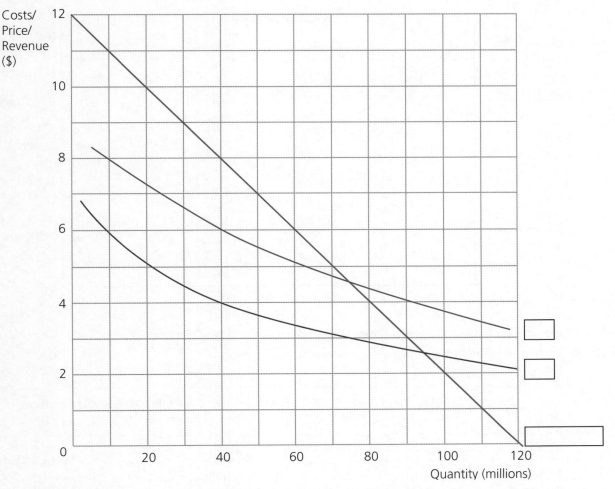

Costs/Price/Revenue ($) — vertical axis, Quantity (millions) — horizontal axis

a On the graph appropriately label all the curves and then identify the equilibrium level of output as **Qm** and identify the equilibrium price as **Pm**. Draw in an accurate MR curve and shade and label the profit made.

b Calculate (and show your working):

(i) the total revenue received by the phone company. _____

(ii) the total cost. _____

(iii) the amount of profit. _____

(iv) the amount of consumer surplus. _____

c Define 'natural monopoly'.

_____

_____

_____

_____

_____

d On the graph identify the price a government could set to achieve normal profit. Label the price as **Pn** and quantity as **Qn**. Shade in the deadweight loss.

4 a Use the graph to answer the questions that follow. Draw an appropriately positioned average cost curve (label it AC) for the firm.

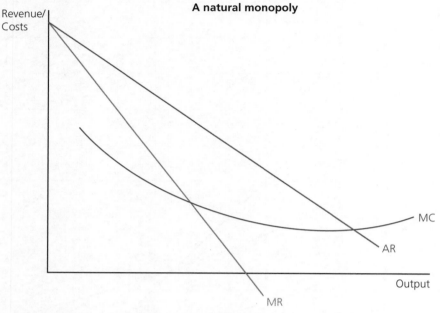

A natural monopoly

b (i) Identify and label the socially desirable price (Pd) and quantity (Qd).

(ii) Explain why the firm is unlikely to produce at this position.

_____

c Describe a government policy that could be used to achieve the socially desirable level of output.

_____

_____

d Label the equilibrium output as price Pmax and quantity Qmax. Shade the area of deadweight loss that results if the natural monopoly produces at the equilibrium level of output. Why is the equilibrium level of output less socially desirable than producing at Qd?

_____

_____

_____

e Indicate if the statements are correct or incorrect.

(i) A natural monopoly's key feature is that it owns patents that protect it from its competitors.	
(ii) A key feature of a natural monopoly is low establishment costs of setting up.	
(iii) A natural monopoly is when the government must grant the right to be a monopoly by statute.	
(iv) A natural monopoly must always earn supernormal profit.	
(v) A natural monopoly will always produce at a level where P = MC.	
(vi) A natural monopoly is when one firm can supply the entire market at lower prices than two or more other firms.	
(vii) A key feature of a natural monopoly is that it will be state owned.	
(viii) A firm is a natural monopoly if its average cost curve falls throughout its relevant output range.	
(ix) A natural monopoly always charges the highest possible price for its product.	
(x) A natural monopoly key feature is high establishment costs and some sort of infrastructure and network.	

5 Market failure can result in underproduction and overpricing for a natural monopoly.

Explain market failure with reference to a natural monopoly. In your answer you should use the graph and:

- Draw an appropriately positioned AR curve and label it AR = P = D. Label the profit maximising price **Pn** and quantity **Qn**. Shade and label the profit made. Label the DWL. To improve resource allocation the government has set the price to equal average cost. Label the price position **Pac** and quantity **Qac**.

- Explain why a price set to equal average cost is more socially desirable than the profit maximising output position and the effect on resource allocation.

- Evaluate the effectiveness of average price controls as a government measure to improve resource allocation in a market controlled by a natural monopoly.

_____

_____

_____

_____

_____

_____

_____

_____

_____

_____

_____

_____

_____

_____

_____

_____

25

THE LONG-RUN POSITION

Monopoly and perfect competition

A monopolist (monopoly) is an imperfect market structure where there is a single seller of a good or service for which there are few, if any, substitutes, while in perfect competition there are many sellers of an identical (homogeneous) product.

Monopolies have strong barriers to entry while in perfect competition there are no barriers to entry and there is perfect knowledge or information. Perfect information (or perfect knowledge) is when consumers and producers in the market system are well informed so they are able to make rational decisions about the use of resources. This means producers are fully informed about the best and most efficient means of production. For consumers this requires that they are fully aware of the price and quantity of goods and service.

The demand curve faced by an individual firm in perfect competition is different from the market demand curve. The firm's demand curve is just one of the individual demand curves of firms that make up the market demand for the industry. The individual seller may sell as much as it wishes of its own production at the market price because the quantity it can supply to the market only has a negligible effect on market price. The demand curve faced by an individual firm is horizontal (perfectly elastic demand) because the firm is too small to influence price and is a price taker. Therefore, the firm's demand curve is not the same as the market demand curve. The market demand curve is determined by the overall demand for the whole market and is downward sloping since it represents the sum of all individual curves, i.e., showing that additional total quantities will only be purchased at lower prices. Because a monopoly is a single seller (producer) the demand curve it faces is the entire market demand curve, which is a downward sloping demand curve as per the law of demand.

The marginal revenue curves for a monopolist and perfectly competitive firm differ. In perfect competition firms are price takers because they are too small to influence price. Because all goods or services are sold for the same price (P) the average revenue (AR) will be equal to the marginal revenue (MR). A monopolist can only increase sales by decreasing the price on all commodities sold therefore marginal revenue (MR) will always be less than the price (P) or average revenue (AR). Therefore, in perfect competition AR = MR while AR is greater than MR for a monopolist (monopoly).

The equilibrium (profit maximising or loss minimising) level of output for both the perfect competitor and the monopolist is where marginal revenue equals marginal cost (MC = MR). The perfect competitor is a price taker but the monopolist can control the price or quantity sold. The marginal revenue is less than the average revenue for the monopolist and therefore the market output will be less and the price will be higher than for perfect competition (ceteris paribus). Pricing for a perfect competitor will involve marginal cost pricing. This is a situation in which price is equal to marginal cost. Sellers cannot charge higher prices, i.e., mark-up price over cost, because they would immediately lose sales to competitors. This is called marginal cost pricing and occurs only in perfect competition. Pricing for a monopolist involves mark up pricing. This is a situation where output is determined from MR = MC, but in which AR and P exceed MC. Sellers are able to charge a price in excess of marginal cost (P > MC). The price is marked up and this is a situation common in a monopoly market.

A monopoly is deemed to restrict output, charge a higher price and sell less than in perfect competition. A perfect competitor would have a lower price and greater quantity when compared with a monopolist. The outcome that is favoured by consumers is assumed to be that under perfect competition because this outcome is allocatively efficient. Therefore, a monopolist imposes a deadweight loss on society because it produces too little output at a higher price.

Long-run equilibriums

A monopolist is able to make and retain supernormal profit in the long run because strong barriers to entry prevent other firms from entering the market and increasing supply, which will move prices down and so eliminate the supernormal profit. A perfect competitive firm cannot earn supernormal profits in the long run because there are no barriers to entry, therefore other firms will enter the industry resulting in an increase in market supply and a fall in price until normal profits are made in the long run.

The rule for maximising profit or minimising a loss is that the most profitable output or smallest loss is where marginal revenue (MR) = marginal cost (MC). Any other position will result in a smaller profit or greater loss.

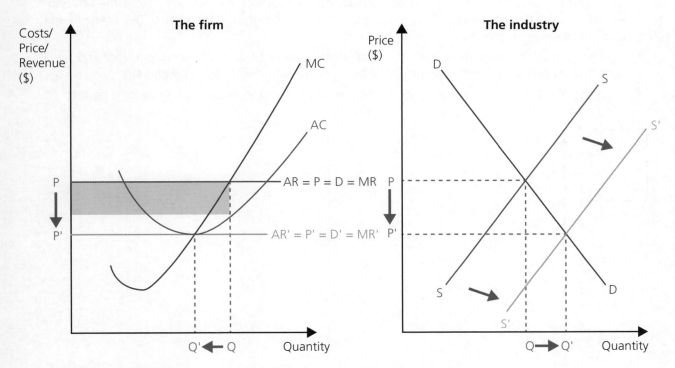

In **perfect competition** the long-run situation is one of normal profits where MR = MC and AR = AC. This is demonstrated by the following analysis. In the diagram the firm is making a supernormal profit at the equilibrium output positon Q. A supernormal profit is a return more than sufficient to keep the entrepreneur in its present activity. Supernormal profits attract other operators into the industry because there are no barriers to entry in perfect competition. Therefore, market supply for the industry will increase from S to S′ causing market price to fall from P to P′. Overall in the market, quantity increases from Q to Q′. Individual firms will now receive P′, make normal profits, this is the long-run equilibrium position. Because supernormal profits are eliminated, it removes the incentive for new operators to enter the industry.

QUESTIONS & TASKS

1 Equilibrium output for a natural monopoly and a perfect competitor are comparable.

Compare and contrast the output for perfect competition and a natural monopoly. In your answer you should:

- Complete the diagram by drawing in an accurate AR curve. Label the vertical axis and the MC and AC curves. Use dotted lines to identify the profit maximising output (**Q**) and price (**P**). Shade in and label the supernormal profit.

- On your completed diagram, identify the price a government could set to achieve a price and output comparable to what a competitive industry would achieve. Label it **Pg** and **Qg**.

- Compare and contrast the output and pricing decisions of a monopolist with those of a perfect competitor.

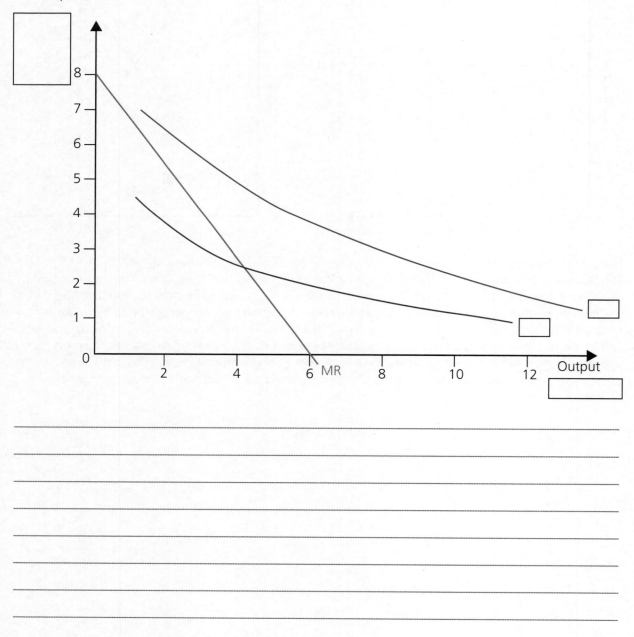

_____

_____

_____

_____

_____

_____

_____

_____

_____

_____

       ISBN: 9780170438117

2 Complete the statements using the diagrams provided.

a At $100 (using AR = P = D = MR):

profit equals _____ and will _____ new firms and supply will _____ and

price _____

b At $50 (using AR' = P' = D' = MR'):

profit is _____ and the incentive for new firms to enter is _____,

because any further increase in _____ and fall in price will see firms make a

_____ profit.

c What are the characteristics of a firm competing in a perfectly competitive industry?

_____

_____

_____

_____

d Define 'normal profit'.

_____

_____

_____

e Explain why a perfectly competitive firm cannot earn supernormal profits in the long run.

_____

_____

_____

_____

3 Use the diagram to answer the questions that follow.

Graph 1

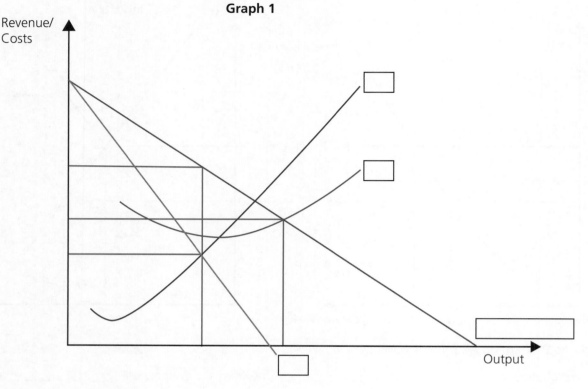

a On Graph 1:

   (i) Label the curves using the small boxes provided.

   (ii) Identify and label the quantity (**Qm**) and price (**Pm**) at which the monopolist will produce.

   (iii) Identify and label the equilibrium quantity (**Qp**) and price (**Pp**) that would occur if the market was perfectly competitive.

   (iv) Shade and label the deadweight loss (DWL) that results from the market being supplied by a monopolist, rather than by perfect competition.

b In Graph 1 the monopolist is making a supernormal profit at monopoly equilibrium.

   (i) Shade and label the supernormal profit.

   (ii) Explain why a monopolist is able to make a supernormal profit in the long run.

   _____

   _____

   _____

c What is one disadvantage to society of a firm being a monopoly?

   _____

   _____

   _____

d Suggest one advantage to society if the government were to grant a license to only one operator to run deep sea mining.

   _____

   _____

4 Use the diagrams to answer the questions that follow.

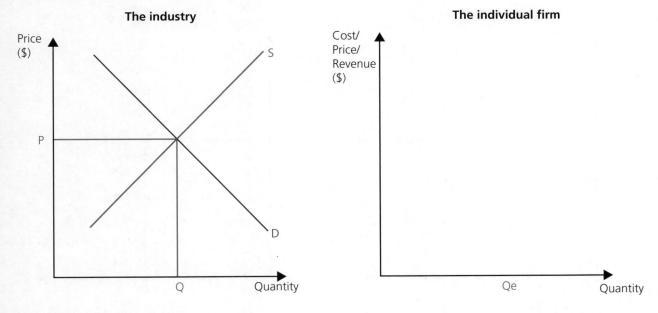

The industry

Price ($)

P

Q   Quantity

The individual firm

Cost/ Price/ Revenue ($)

Qe   Quantity

a Draw on the appropriate diagram an AC and MC curve to show the individual firm making normal profits at Qe.

b Show the effect of an increase in the number of firms starting up business. Label the new equilibrium P1 and Q1 on both diagrams.

c Assuming that there are no changes in costs faced by individual firms, shade in the level of profits now earned by each firm.

d Explain why a perfect competitor faces a horizontal AR curve.

_____

_____

_____

_____

_____

_____

_____

_____

_____

_____

_____

_____

_____

_____

_____

5 Use the diagram to answer the questions that follow.

The individual firm

The industry

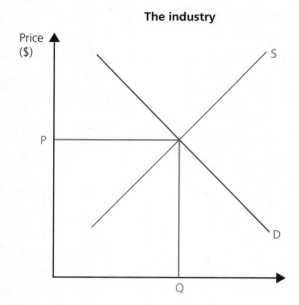

a On the appropriate diagram draw in average total costs to illustrate farmers making normal profits. Show the output as Qd.

b On both diagrams show what would have happened from increased demand (label both diagrams fully). Explain what has happened to the individual firm regarding:

(i) Profit (and shade this in): _____

(ii) Output: _____

(iii) Price: _____

c A perfectly competitive firm has marginal revenue of $2.50. The level of output is currently 10 000 units. Calculate:

(i) total revenue $_____

(ii) average revenue $_____

d List four characteristics of a perfectly competitive firm that could apply to a dairy farm.

_____

_____

_____

_____

_____

_____

_____

_____

6 In perfect competition an individual firm produces a small fraction of total output and cannot influence market price.

Explain features of perfect competition. In your answer you should:

- On Graph 2 label all the curves appropriately, using the small boxes for answers.
- Explain how Graph 1 and Graph 2 illustrate perfectly competitive competition.
- On Graph 2 clearly label the equilibrium level of output as Qm. Show and label appropriately the amount of supernormal or subnormal profit being made at this level of output. Clearly label the shutdown point (S) and break-even point (B).
- Explain why the firm may continue to produce in the short run even if the price temporarily falls below the break-even price.
- On both Graph 1 and Graph 2 show the long-run equilibrium situation.

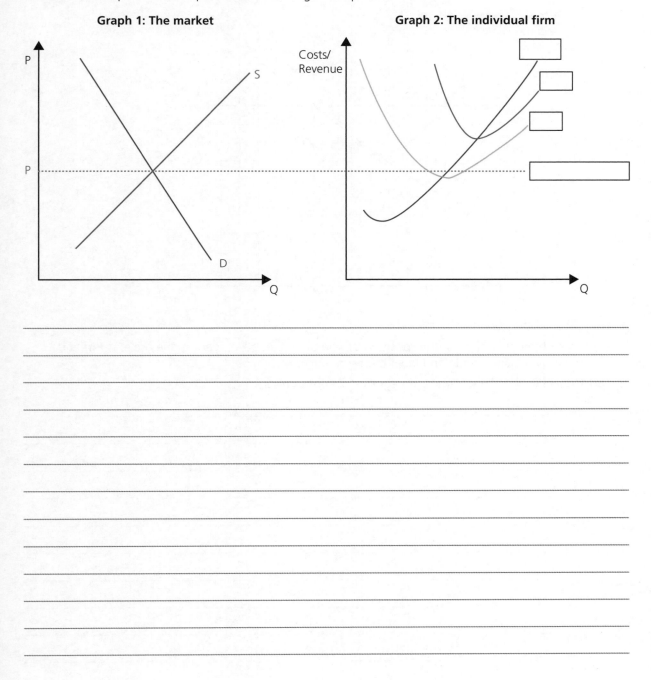

Graph 1: The market

Graph 2: The individual firm

_____
_____
_____
_____
_____
_____
_____
_____
_____
_____
_____
_____
_____
_____
_____
_____

Question one: Long-run perfect competition

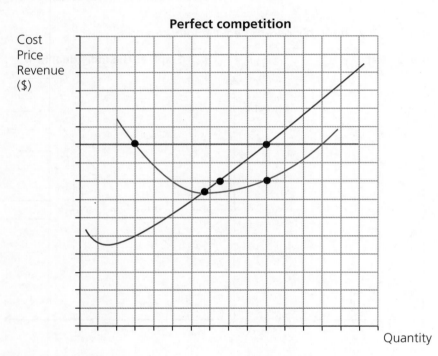

Perfect competition

Cost
Price
Revenue
($)

Quantity

a **(i)** Label all the curves.

(ii) Show the equilibrium output position on the diagram above, identify the price as **Pm** and quantity as **Qm**. Shade and label the economic profit made.

(iii) Explain in detail why Qm is the equilibrium position.

_____

_____

_____

_____

_____

_____

_____

_____

_____

_____

_____

_____

b **(i)** On the diagram on the previous page label the long-run equilibrium position, identify the price as **Pe** and quantity as **Qe**.

(ii) Using marginal analysis explain the changes on your diagram.

_____

_____

_____

_____

_____

_____

_____

_____

_____

_____

_____

_____

_____

_____

_____

_____

_____

_____

_____

_____

_____

_____

_____

_____

_____

_____

_____

_____

_____

_____

_____

_____

_____

_____

Question two: Allocative efficiency

a Explain equilibrium output for firms. In your answer you should:

- Calculate the values of the missing items in the table and put them in the spaces provided. Firm A is a perfect competitor and Firm B is a monopoly.
- Make a recommendation on the action they should follow to maximise profits. Justify your position.

	Price (P)	Marginal Revenue (MR)	Quantity (Q)	Total Revenue (TR)	Total Cost (TC)	Average Cost (AC)	Marginal Cost (MC)
Firm A	$1.50		100		$150		$2.00
Firm B		$1.50	1 000	$2 000	$1 750		$1.50

Firm A: _____

_____

_____

_____

_____

_____

_____

_____

Firm B: _____

_____

_____

_____

_____

_____

_____

_____

_____

_____

_____

_____

_____

_____

_____

_____

_____

_____

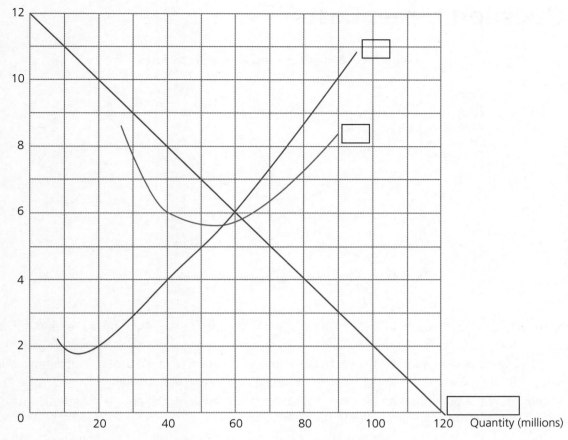

Costs/
Price/
Revenue
($)

Quantity (millions)

b (i) On the diagram appropriately label all the curves and then identify the equilibrium level of output as **Qm** and identify the equilibrium price as **Pm**. Draw in an accurate **MR** curve and shade and label the profit made.

(ii) Label the perfect competition price (**Pp**) and quantity (**Qp**).

(iii) Using the distinguishing feature of a monopoly, explain why a deadweight loss exists.

(iv) Using the distinguishing feature of a perfectly competitive firm, explain why it is allocatively efficient.

Question three: Costs

A perfect competitor – increase in fixed costs

a (i) On the diagram, label the cost curves, identify the profit maximising price (**Pe**) and quantity (**Qe**).

(ii) Draw a new average cost curve (**AC2**) to reflect an increase in fixed costs. Shade in and label the new profit made in the short run (normal, subnormal or supernormal).

(iii) Show the effect that an increase in fixed costs will have on the price (**Pc**) and quantity (**Qc**) in the long run, label any curve shifts that will occur.

(iv) Using the distinguishing features of perfect competition explain the change in the market that takes place over the two time periods. Refer to marginal analysis and the diagram in your answer.

_____

_____

_____

_____

_____

_____

_____

_____

_____

_____

_____

_____

_____

_____

_____

_____

_____

_____

_____

       ISBN: 9780170438117

A perfect competitor – decrease in variable costs

Cost
Price
Revenue

AR = MR = D = P

Quantity

b (i) On the diagram, label the cost curves, identify the profit maximising price (**Pk**) and quantity (**Qk**).

(ii) Draw a new average cost curve (AC3) and marginal cost curve (MC2) to reflect a decrease in variable costs. Shade in and label the new profit made in the short run (normal, subnormal or supernormal).

(iii) Show the effect that a decrease in variable costs will have on the price (Pn) and quantity (Qn) in the long run, and label any curve shifts that will occur.

(iv) Using the distinguishing features of perfect competition explain the change in the market that takes place over the two time periods. Refer to marginal analysis and the diagram in your answer.

_____

_____

_____

_____

_____

_____

_____

_____

_____

_____

_____

_____

_____

_____

_____

_____

_____

_____

_____

Question four: Monopoly

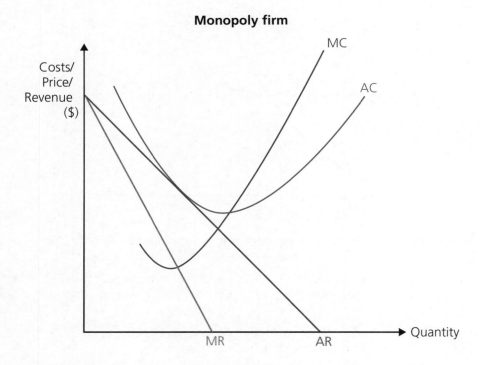

Monopoly firm

a (i) Using MR and AR identify the profit maximising price (**P1**) and quantity (**Q1**).

(ii) Show an increase in market demand as indicated by **MR2**, label the new demand as **AR2**. Label the new profit maximising price (**P2**) and quantity (**Q2**). Shade in and label the profit made.

(iii) Using marginal analysis explain the impact on price, profit and output decisions of the monopolist.

_____

_____

_____

_____

_____

_____

_____

_____

_____

_____

_____

_____

_____

_____

_____

_____

_____

_____

Monopoly firm

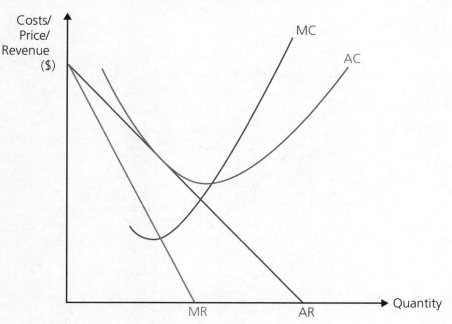

b (i) Using MR and AR identify the profit maximising price (**Pe**) and quantity (**Qe**).

(ii) Show an increase in variable costs. Label the new profit maximising price (**Pe2**) and quantity (**Qe2**). Shade in and label the profit made.

(iii) Using marginal analysis explain the impact on price, profit and output decisions of the monopolist.

_____

_____

_____

_____

_____

_____

_____

_____

_____

_____

_____

_____

_____

_____

Question five: Natural monopoly and allocative efficiency

A natural monopoly – equilibrium output

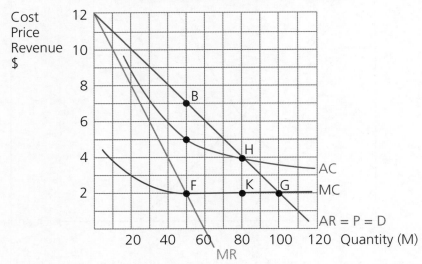

a **(i)** Show the equilibrium output position on the diagram, identify the price as **Pe** and quantity as **Qe**.

(ii) Explain in detail why Qe is the equilibrium position.

(iii) Shade and label the profit and deadweight loss at Qe.

_____

_____

_____

_____

_____

_____

_____

_____

_____

_____

_____

_____

_____

_____

_____

_____

_____

_____

_____

_____

_____

A natural monopoly – marginal cost pricing

b (i) Show the equilibrium output position on the diagram if the government enforced marginal cost pricing. Identify the price as **Pm** and quantity as **Qm**.

(ii) Explain in detail the impact on allocative efficiency of Pm.

(iii) Use shading to illustrate further intervention that may be needed if the government uses marginal cost pricing. Explain why this intervention is required.

_____

_____

_____

_____

_____

_____

_____

_____

_____

_____

_____

_____

_____

_____

_____

_____

_____

_____

_____

_____

_____

_____

A natural monopoly – average cost pricing

c **(i)** Show the equilibrium output position on the diagram if the government enforced average cost pricing. Identify the price as **Pa** and quantity as **Qa**.

(ii) Explain in detail the impact on allocative efficiency of Pa. Shade and label in any loss in allocative efficiency if average cost pricing is used.

(iii) Explain why average cost pricing is more effective than marginal cost pricing.

_____

_____

_____

_____

_____

_____

_____

_____

_____

_____

_____

_____

_____

_____

_____

_____

_____

_____

_____

_____

_____

_____

_____

   ISBN: 9780170438117

_____
_____
_____
_____
_____
_____
_____
_____
_____
_____
_____
_____

Question six

In the long run a perfect competitor will earn normal profits.

Explain why perfectly competitive firms make normal profit in the long run. In your answer you should:

- On Graph 1 below label the profit maximising level of output as **Qe** and shade and label the area of subnormal profit made.
- Explain why the marginal revenue curve for a perfectly competitive firm is drawn as a horizontal line.
- Explain why farmers who entered the dairy industry at the height of the 'boom' face the greatest risk of failure.
- Assuming this firm remains in the industry for the long run, explain how its profit maximising level of output will change.

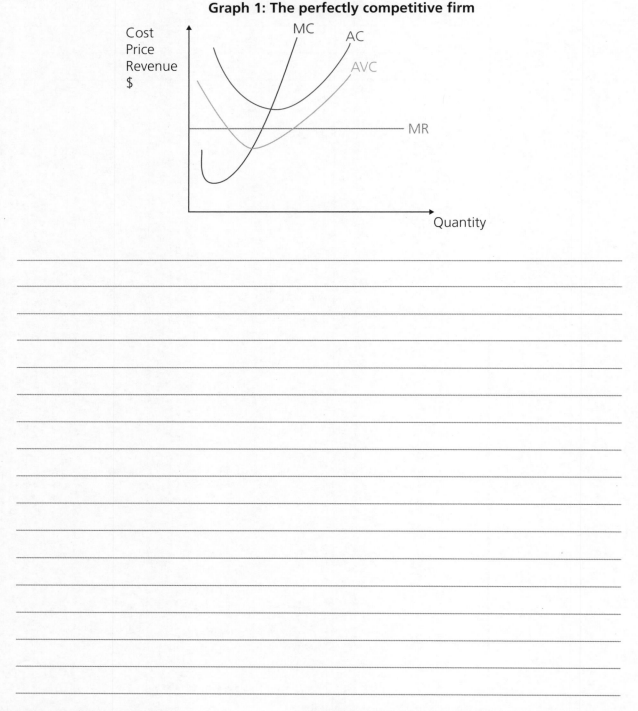

Graph 1: The perfectly competitive firm

Cost
Price
Revenue
$

MC

AC

AVC

MR

Quantity

_____
_____
_____
_____
_____
_____
_____
_____
_____
_____
_____
_____
_____
_____
_____
_____
_____
_____

 ISBN: 9780170438117